My Life In Thought & Poem

KEITH A. BRIDGES

Mountain Move, LLC

MY LIFE IN THOUGHT & POEM

CONTENTS

This book is dedicated to my wife, Beverly.

Without her encouragement, this book would not have been started and, by no means, would it ever have been finished. Countless times I had to stop her in the middle of her projects, reading, and housework to ask for help in spelling and English composition. Now, there will be some areas where the English may still not be the best but, as the old saying goes, that just comes with the territory.

Then, I would like to thank my many friends for being so kind and for letting me get by with using some of them in my poems. That is what good friends are for, is it not? - To be able to take a joke and put up with guys like me.

I want to thank my children and grandchildren, and my brothers and sisters for giving me such needed inspiration, some sad, and of course, some humorous. Without them, a lot of these poems would never have been written, and some of my family heritage would never have been recorded.

This is really what my book is all about...
My life, my thoughts, my family, and my friends.

~ One ~

MY LIFE

Section Contents

Finished

Well, I have finally done it,
My book is now complete.
I tried to make it different,
And make it rather neat.

I've included friends and family,
My wife and children, too.
To all of you, my grandchildren,
A section, just for you.

I've recorded thoughts and history,
Things that most times, fade away.
I have put them down on paper,
Just for you to read someday.

This is my contribution,
That I will leave with you.
Perhaps you'll take time to read it,
When you have nothing else to do.

-Keith

Beyond our control we are caught up

in a vortex of emotions, having

little control over the myriad

of circumstances that

we will encounter.

**They may as well be put into a
Book of Poems**

A Book of Poems

There is something about a book of poems,
That is bound to catch one's eye.
So write a book of poems, I thought,
Is something I should try.

Some things will be rather humorous,
Some things will be food for thought.
The English may not be the best,
But read them, *Oh, you ought!*

For I wrote them to give you pleasure,
In a world that is full of doubt.
From the beginning of my early life,
Is what my book is all about.

I do hope that you enjoy,
The things that you will read.
So sit back, relax, and enjoy yourself,
Isn't that what everybody needs?

It is such an awesome thought when I think about it. Upon conception, I became a living soul to begin my journey down life's road, not knowing what would lie ahead and having very little control over the events that would become *my life.*

We live for what feels like a few short years, getting caught up in the whirlwind of our daily lives. Then, in a blink, our life on earth will come to a close...and our new life in eternity begins.

The choices I make along the way, are mine to make. I alone can choose to trust God. To trust that He has a plan for me as I walk down *Life's Road.*

Life's Road

We are ushered into this life,
By God's almighty hand.
And life for you and life for me,
At that moment just began.

We cannot tell what lies ahead,
From the rising to the setting of the sun.
The heartaches we have, the joys we share,
Are not the same for everyone.

God has a special plan for us,
As we travel down life's road.
For some it will seem a life of ease,
For others, a constant heavy load.

But these are not the things we question,
We must trust, God understands.
And we accept the things He gives us,
Until life's road comes to an end.

My Family -- We lived in Greenfield, Ohio when this picture was taken. My sister Eleanor was away at the time staying with friends of the family, the Bush's. My mother is holding Phillip. Jimmy and Judy were not yet born. Our tiny brother, Bernard had died when he was just a small baby. Counting all with Mom and Dad, that makes seventeen!

My Family

Although I cannot prove it,
This is the way it seems to me.
My dad, he probably caught her eye,
And was just as ornery as could be.

My mom was probably kind of weak,
Her face turned pink with blush.
And people all around, they squirmed,
At that certain kind of mush.

Well, one thing led to another,
And propose to Mom, Dad did.
And naturally what happened next,
There came this batch of kids.

First, a little boy named Arthur,
A story later on you will read.
So I'll just go on to the next,
To pick up a little speed.

Then came brother Bernard,
A little guy frail and not so good.
Soon to be returned to Jesus.
To go home so soon, God knew he would.

My sister Marge was number three,
The delight and what a thrill.
Little did my dad know what lay ahead,
You see, back then, there was no pill!

Then Lois was born in eighteen months,
Or close to that, I think.
Now she's the one that would grow up,
To be an ornery little fink.

Well, another little girl was born,
The one they called Eleanor June.
She would grow up a fine young girl,
And grow up she did too soon.

Then Paul was born, "Another boy,"
My dad said, with much relief.
"I'm certainly glad to see you, Bud."
My mom said, "Oh, good grief!"

It wasn't long then after that,
Another boy, named Joe.
A happy boy he would always be,
I think God had willed it so.

Well, things had kind of settled down,
Mom decided to take a break.
And Dad, he certainly did agree,
This was almost more than he could take.

Now if you can take this sudden jolt,
There came this set of twins.
By now the house was full of kids,
For beds, they were using the sugar bins.

My mom said, "Ralph, we've got to stop.
I just don't know what to do."
My dad said, "Ah, we went this far,
Why not one more or even two?"

Well, first let's tag these little guys,
So we will always know.
Which one is Keith, which one is Kenny,
And they tagged us up just so.

Now they could have taken a little more time,
But it wasn't long at that.
Along came little brother Bob,
All big and round and fat.

Now, let us see, who was next,
Oh yes, Norma was her name.
To me it was just another girl,
By now they all looked just the same.

Wouldn't you have thought that they were through?
Goodness, there's other things that people do.
But Carole came, I kid you not,
Before the last was off the pot.

Okay, Phillip, it is now your turn,
To face the Bridges tribe.
Come right on in and join the crowd,
You can just sit here by my side.

What I am about to tell you now,
Is going to blow your mind.
We're not done yet, there's more to come,
They're just lagging a little behind.

Now Jim was kind of special,
Because he came a little late.
"Don't panic now," my sister said,
"We'll just put on another plate."

You've heard the old, old saying,
There is always room for more.
And if we lack a chair or two,
We'll simply dump him on the floor.

Now, if you can just bear with me,
I am almost done, you see.
My mom was close to forty-nine,
How many more could there be?

To have one more would be just great,
There was no choice, it was too late.
Poor Dad, he thought that he was through,
"Just name her Judy," he said, "That's what we'll do."

So there you have the history,
And the story of our clan.
You will agree with me, I think,
My dad was... quite a man!

Judy & Jimmy

While I have your attention, I want to tell you... all those things
you've heard about those preachers' kids?? Well, they are true!

It probably started when I was less than a year old. This story was told by my mother and this is the way I will always remember it...

Who Won The Race?

There is a town in Ohio called Sidney,
And a street named Orbison Hill.
I was too young to remember living there,
But I was told, that's where I got my first thrill.

My mother had made a major purchase,
And brought home two shiny new pots.
She placed them on the floor in the hallway,
"For the twins," she said, "for the rest they are not."

There we were, my twin brother and I,
What a thrill and what a delight.
Sitting on our shiny new potties,
Getting ready for our first race that night.

Now, I don't remember who was the first,
To shove off and lead down the hall.
But my family was watching and laughing,
To see who would beat, after all.

There is no way now I could prove it,
Time has passed, I wouldn't know how.
As far as I am concerned, my twin brother,
I beat you by a country mile.

p.s. What's that old saying, Kenny?
Either do something or get off the pot!

We left Sidney, Ohio and moved several times after that. Around 1939, or it could have been 1940, we moved to the small town of Fletcher, Ohio. There my dad bought a small 8-acre farm on the east side of town about two city blocks from the railroad tracks and the local grain elevator. It wasn't a big farm, but it was big enough to raise a bunch of kids and for ornery preacher's kids to get into trouble and just try to cover most of their tracks and, above all, their sins. Well, I thought so anyway. But you can count on it... *Your sins will find you out!*

Your Sins Will Find You Out

In a little town called Fletcher,
My dad bought a plot of ground.
A place to plant some corn and beans,
And for a dozen kids to play around.

We had some cows and chickens,
We had some rabbits and some pigs.
We set aside a truck patch,
It was a place to plant and dig.

We planted peas and carrots,
And kept out all the weeds.
And in this certain corner,
We always planted melon seeds.

When the melons started growing,
On them my dad would keep an eye.
"I always cut the first," he said.
One day I thought, *Why not I?*

So I got a knife quite big and sharp,
And whacked a melon from the vine.
And then I cut it open,
Oh my, it tasted oh so fine.

And then I sort of panicked,
And said, "What shall I do?"
"I'll have to bury the seeds," I thought,
"I'll bury all, not just a few."

So in the center of the cornfield,
I found a real nice spot.
I dug a hole and buried all,
Man, I was dumber than I thought.

Naturally, the seeds started growing,
And much to Dad's surprise.
Yes sir, out there in the cornfield,
Melons growing right before his eyes.

Now my dad was kind of cagey,
Sometimes he would just let things go.
That is, until the time was perfect,
To let everybody know.

Then came the right occasion,
My dad came waltzing through the door.
His hands were full of melon vines,
I nearly passed out on the floor.

"I found these in the cornfield,"
My dad said, without a doubt.
"Now, it doesn't matter which one did it,
But remember - Your sins will *always*
Find   You   Out!"

And then there was...

The Electric Fence

One day my father approached me,
With a chore that had to be done.
"We have to string up an electric fence," he said,
"And it has to be done by one."

"For I bought a cow from a farmer,
And he's bringing her here in his truck.
At one is the time he will be here.
But we should be ready, *with a lot of luck.*"

Well, I got the wire and the staples,
My brother got the digger and poles.
My dad went to town for the electric charger,
And we started digging the holes.

The job couldn't have gone any better,
Everything was set and ready to go.
Down the lane came the cow and the farmer,
I ran and told Dad, so he would know.

We put the cow in the pasture,
Yet something just didn't seem right.
Oh no! My brother hadn't tested the charger,
And it had to be tested that night.

I tried to get my brother to touch it,
"What kind of fool do you take me to be?!
You touch it if you wanna see if it's working,
And I'll just sit back and see."

Well, we both came to one conclusion,
Neither one was as dumb as all that.
So we threw the switch on the charger,
And pondered the situation as we sat.

And then the idea did hit me,
I tied the cow's tail to the wire.
As I threw the switch on the charger,
All you could smell was hair and see fire.

The poor old cow just kept running,
To stop her, my dad said I must.
But all you could see was the barbed wire,
Among the hair and the dust.

Well, I cut her tail from the barbed wire,
And got her calmed down a bit.
My dad said, "I'm gonna teach you one good lesson, boy,
Now you just grab hold of it!"

It seemed as if there was always some excitement going on in that small town and, if there wasn't any excitement going on, you can bet this young hobbledehoy was about to make some. Gosh, I remember one day... *Here goes poor brother Bob again, he was so respectful, but it seemed as if I was always getting in trouble with him.* Well, anyway, Bob came running out across the yard to where I was. I'm not going to tell you what I was doing; maybe someday later on I will.

Bob said, "Look! Over there across the fields something is on fire!" Out across the fields of wheat, there was this huge billow of black smoke bellowing toward the sky. "Let's go find out what is going on," Bob said. Man, I don't know if I should tell you this or not, but I guess someday the secret is bound to get out some way or the other, so I may as well go ahead and tell you. Hmm, I wonder... *Is the scar still there?*

Is the Scar Still There

"The furniture store is burning!"
My brother Bob called out to me.
"Let's hitch a ride and go to town,
So we can better see."

We beat it down the back ally,
To the main street that ran through town.
We were standing there hitching us a ride,
Pushing, shoving, and horsing around.

Down the street came this mean old lady,
Now she was toting all her bags.
Brother Bob started poking fun,
And even called her an old hag.

"That isn't nice," I said to him,
"You'll be old yourself one day.
And for all you know, brother Bob,
You'll act yourself that way."

Now I was whittling with my knife,
Upon a stick or two.
"You stop poking fun," I said,
"Or I'll stick my knife in you."

Well brother Bob doesn't learn too fast,
He just kept on poking fun.
So I started after him with my knife,
While he was on the run.

Now brother Bob, he stopped too fast,
I was upon him in a flash.
He hollered, and the blood it ran,
Oh, it was a horrible gash.

Well, I begged him not to panic,
And please never tell Dad what I'd done.
We'd just say it sort of happened,
While we both were out having fun.

Then I ran to the local drugstore,
For some iodine and some gauze.
And I told the druggist not to worry,
It was certainly for a worthy cause.

Poor brother Bob, he had to drop his pants,
Right there on the city street.
I packed the wound all nice and tight,
And wrapped him up real neat.

Oh, I forgot to tell you where I stuck him,
Even though it was so unkind.
Yes, Bob and I will always remember,
It was right in his...behind!

*Man, what kids won't do! I checked with my brother Bob,
and yes, the scar was still there!*

*I know, you are still wondering if my dad really made me grab hold of
The Electric Fence. Aren't you? Now you honestly don't think I shake and
stammer because I was born this way, do you?*

There are so many childhood stories that I could share with you and maybe some day in a sequel, I will. But for now, I would like to take you a few years into my life as a very young teenager and share with you a portion of that time. We all have our trials, testing, and heartaches in life; that is just the way it will always be. Most of them we will never understand, and some will have lasting effects on our lives for years to come. Some of them we think we will never get over, no matter how many years go by, but memory has a way of fading into a vapor, a thing of the past, but yet... *the hurting never stops.*

In the morning, I watched Art's plane fly in circles high above my head.
Little did I know the events that were to follow that evening.

And there it was, as big as life, as big as big could be.
This great big plane came flying in, right there for all to see.

The Hurting Never Stops

I'm going to tell you a story,
That's as true as true can be.
I'm not quite certain of the date,
I think near nineteen forty-three.

But it was in the summertime,
I was standing in the yard.
And you could hear this humming sound,
If you listened real, real hard.

Then there it was, as big as life,
As big as big could be.
This great big plane came flying in,
For everyone to see.

It hummed aloft, in circles flew,
And we all danced about.
Someone yelled, "It's brother Art!"
And there wasn't any doubt.

Now he had bought this airplane,
Down in Texas way.
And for some unknown reason,
Had decided to fly home that day.

Then as we watched him high above,
He headed for the west.
He knew a field in which to land,
It was a place that he knew best.

The moments passed, my brother came,
Driving up the narrow road.
He stopped the car and then got out,
He looked so big and bold.

He had a grin from ear to ear,
And one could plainly see.
He had a surprise for everyone,
And I knew he had one for even me.

Art and Dad exchanged greetings,
My mom just stood there with a smile.
And yet there was something eerie,
You could just feel it all the while.

"I'm going to take you all a ride,"
My brother said to me.
"She's a good old plane, she'll hold one,
Well maybe two or even three."

We all piled into the family car,
Packed in real good and tight.
And headed for that landing strip,
For the first and final flight.

There it sat, all big and shiny,
A wondrous sight to see.
I can still remember how I felt,
And the effects it had on me.

My brother turned and said to Dad,
"You are the first to go."
My dad glanced at my brother, Paul,
The disappointment began to show.

"Aw, you go ahead and take your turn,
I'll follow when you're done.
For after all there's lots of time,
And a ride for everyone."

My brother, Paul, got on the wing,
And stood there big and tall.
Just look at me he seemed to say,
I'm going to show you all.

He must have spotted Joseph,
Standing there so meek.
Now Joe could tear your heart right out,
He didn't even have to speak.

I really don't remember now,
But Joe was in the plane.
And the engine started humming,
Then everything just went insane.

The plane was in the air,
And sort of hung there in the sky.
My sister screamed, my brother ran,
My dad sobbed, "Please God, don't let them die."

The plane then fell from heaven's loft,
Right there for all to see.
I cried, I ran, through blinded tears,
It seemed like an eternity.

The flames, it seemed, were everywhere,
And people running all about.
But hope was gone, the boys were dead,
There wasn't any doubt.

My father desperately tried to reach them,
But his efforts were in vain.
I could see the charred bodies sitting,
In the ruins of the plane.

The earth trembled with explosions,
Black smoke bellowed toward the sky.
And I cried out in horror,
"Would someone, please, tell me why?!"

A farmer friend was standing by,
And gently took me by the hand.
"I know it hurts son, it always will,
But just try and understand."

Well, I do not understand it,
And I never will, I guess.
But God always has a reason,
And I know that He knows what is best.

There seemed to be a hundred questions why, but there never was an answer. Joe was only fifteen years old, and Art was twenty-eight. I remember going out that night to milk one of the cows; the chores still had to be done, no matter what the events of the day were.

I was still in a state of shock. I felt as if I were just dreaming and I would soon wake up. Everything was such a blur, and I just kept seeing Art's plane falling from the sky and bursting into flames. Dad trying to get to the plane to get the boys out, Paul pulling on Dad's arm dragging him away from the burning plane, a farmer with such sadness in his eyes helping dad find a place to sit down, and not being able to comfort him. It was all so very sad.

As I leaned my head into the side of the cow to milk, I sobbed. As a young teenage Christian I remember thinking with such anguish, and I could have said it out loud, "Jesus, why? …You control every-thing. This just doesn't make sense. Why would you let this happen? Why the heartache? Why Joe?"

I guess I felt that way because he was the one closest to me. I sat there milking, then I finished the chores that had to be done and pondered over the horrible events of the day.

Nevertheless, one day the storm subsided, a calm settled in, and I continued down *life's road.*

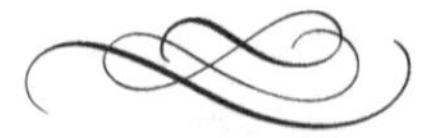

I grew up with all the problems and confusion that most teenagers have. I wasn't any different. I quit school while in the eighth grade and commuted across the fields to work on the farm of a local farmer. Later on, when I was fourteen years old, I went to Pennsylvania and enrolled at a Bible School in Freeport. Three years later I was back home. I took a meager job in a local tool company and struggled to survive.

Because our family was so large and we were so very poor, I really didn't have all that much going for me. But, one day something quite wonderful happened to change all of that. In the small town of Troy, Ohio, I met the girl of my dreams. You have heard the quote, "She has it all." Well, let me tell you, she certainly did have it all. I mean she... okay, okay, I'll drop it. But you were not there. If you had been, you would know what I'm talking about. What she ever saw in this poor preacher's kid, I'll never know. But after a short courtship we, as the old saying goes, *tied the knot.*

Bev and I worked hard to put a home together. We managed, we saved, and we skimped to get ahead. I had strong drives and many goals to achieve. I didn't want my children to be poor like I was. I wanted my wife to have a nice home, a new car to drive, clothes to look her best, and to be able to take vacations and see the world. I wanted my children to have a good education and see them grow up to have nice homes and happy families. These were the things I wanted. These were the dreams I went after. These were the goals I would achieve.

As persistent as I was and with this lifestyle, we were always a church family. We were active in church affairs, going to church every Sunday morning, Sunday night, and on Wednesday nights. We hardly ever missed a revival and went to everything in between. Bev was Director of Children's Ministry and taught Junior Church most of twenty years. I myself spent a good bit of those years right beside her teaching untold hours at the church and working on various projects. My daughter, son-in-law, and I would minister through Musical Art Programs for other churches. Michelle and Stan would sing as I painted in oils and spoke in poetic form.

I am not telling you all of this to impress you with what I did or what I accomplished. That is not the point. What I want you to know is, in the midst of this auspicious, favorable setting, I my friend, was missing the boat. We can be so involved in our lifestyle and in our church activities that we lose all perspective and the greatest gift of all.

I was so concerned about *My House* that I had no time for *My Friend*. - I want to share with you a wonderful thing that happened. It's about **My House, My Friend.**

I have this house with many rooms,
They're spacious and they're fine.

I have a garden with winding paths,

Its beauty to behold...

In the morning, I watch the rising of the sun.

In the evening, its setting in hues of gold.

My House, My Friend

I have this house with many rooms,
They're spacious and they're fine.
I have a place to romp and play,
I have a place to eat and dine.

I have one room just to sit and read,
A room for quiet and rest.
I have a room for little pets,
And a place for birds to nest.

I have a loft that is just for guests,
One room that is big and neat.
It's just to entertain my friends,
To sit around and snack and eat.

I have a garden with winding paths,
Its beauty to behold.
In the morning, I watch the rising of the sun,
In the evening, the setting in hues of gold.

I have an attic that is filled quite full,
With things of value and some things quite rare.
I have a little box locked up real tight,
And in it, only I know what is there.

On my journeys one day while traveling,
I got acquainted with this man.
There was something about Him that touched me,
I thought, I would like Him for my friend.

So I invited Him to come and dine,
And see my spacious home.
I was so proud I could not wait,
Until I got Him there alone.

Once inside, I took His cloak,
And placed it neatly on the rack.
The proper host I was indeed,
There was nothing I did lack.

Impressed, my friend did gaze about,
A smile appeared upon His face.
And with a twinkle in His eye, He said,
"I really like your place."

"Let me show you all my rooms,"
I said with great delight.
"Then we shall dine, and we shall rest,
And you, Sir, shall spend the night."

I took Him to my reading room,
My books all neat and in a row.
"I don't like what you read," He said,
"Most of these will have to go."

I stared at Him and said not a word,
I thought, "After all you are my guest.
If I take you through the other rooms,
Will you also not like *the rest?*"

As we walked along the corridor,
He noticed the pictures on my wall.
"I'd also like those changed," He said,
"They're not what I like, at all."

"Not what you like, sir?" I questioned,
"They fill me with pride and delight.
But so as not to offend you,
I'll remove them from out of your sight."

I approached the dining room with caution,
I knew the feast would be fit for a king.
But, would He like what I set before Him?
So far, He hasn't liked much of anything.

But yet there was something about Him,
That I was willing to yield His way.
And I really wanted Him for my friend,
And at my house each night and day.

We both sat down at the table,
I reached for the meat and the bread.
Then my guest so kindly suggested,
"First, would you please bow your head?"

"You ask me, sir, bow before you,
A guest in my house you are.
Now I really want you for my friend,
But please, sir, don't take this too far."

My friend looked at me with compassion,
"It's not that complicated, you see.
But if you want me a guest in your house,
There are changes that will just have to be."

"Would you show me the rest of your rooms?
I'd like to see what your house is about.
Together we'll make the right changes,
There are things I'll want you to take out."

Together we searched each room,
I removed the things that offended my friend.
I was amazed how willing I yielded,
To each change that He did so demand.

His smile of approval did melt me,
In my house He was taking control.
The bond of our friendship grew stronger,
We were becoming one body and soul.

But when we approached the attic,
I remembered my little box hidden there.
I hoped my new friend wouldn't find it,
For with it, I did not want to share.

Yet that was the first thing He noticed,
The little box I had hidden with care.
Then He asked me to please hand it to Him,
And the key and the contents to share.

"Sir, I brought you as a guest to my house,
I've made changes so we could be friends.
But the little box, I don't want to part with,
You can just have my house and my land."

"What is in the little box that is so precious,
That for our friendship, you'd cast aside?
Please tell me what's under the lock and key."
"Well, sir... It's my *self and my pride.*"

That is when I looked into the mirror of my life and saw myself
for what I really was. - *What is in a mirror?*

What Is In a Mirror

What is in a mirror,
That hangs on a wall?
That spellbinds the mighty,
That amuses the small.

That makes the arrogant,
See what they are not.
That makes the humble,
Ponder in thought.

It causes the deceitful,
Just to stare into space.
Being reminded of the truth,
From the look on their face.

It makes the haughty,
Hang their head in shame.
For they know at one glance,
They have played life's wrong game.

It makes the proud,
See at a glance,
All they have gained,
Is at their own expense.

One searches for the future,
For the things that will last.
But all that is revealed,
Are the things of the past.

What is in a mirror,
That hangs on a wall?
Only the truth is revealed.
That is all.

-And the truth was, that it really was my *self and my pride.* Was I really ready and willing to hand it over?

He stood there one moment before me,
With love and an outstretched hand.
There I placed the little box in surrender,
And then, He became my friend.

Now at last I could fully comprehend the genuine loving nature of God. Not only was He my Father, He now became my friend. After that phenomenal and wonderful encounter when I handed over the *little box* that was so very important to me, the desires I had, the achievements I sought after, and the goals I was seeking... just didn't seem to matter anymore. With self out of the way, I was soon to learn that there are - *Some things I cannot do.*

Some Things I Cannot Do

There are some things I cannot do,
If I am to be God's man.
I cannot claim His promises,
Unless we walk hand in hand.

I cannot go to Him in prayer,
With hidden sins deep in my heart.
I cannot ask Him for His will,
If I have not done my part.

I cannot witness of the truth,
If condemnation reigns within.
I cannot sing His wondrous praise,
If therein dwells this inbred sin.

I cannot enter that sacred room,
Where the Holy Spirit there awaits.
I cannot enter that sacred realm,
If my heart is full of debate.

I cannot ask the King of Kings,
For a place in His eternity,
Unless I meet Him at the cross,
Where there He died for me.

A genuine union had taken place. It was so very important now for me, throughout the day and amidst my busy schedule, to just stop and have some time with Him. To talk to Him and thank Him for His revelation to me at this time in my life. I cannot impress upon you enough what this will mean in your life. It is such a fleeting life span that is allocated to each of us, so, *if it's only a moment...*

If It's Only a Moment

If it's only a moment, just take it,
From every day of your life.
And remind God how much that you love Him,
Take a moment from the toil and strife.

Thank Him for the many things that He gives you,
Then thank him for the many times that He cares.
Oh yes, and never forget to thank Him,
For the way that He answers your prayers.

While you are at it, take a moment to thank Him,
Yes, thank Him for not doubting your trust.
You know what? I think God really needs that.
Yes, I think He needs that from all of us.

He is a God of compassion, we are His,
Redeemed and purchased by love.
So never fail to take those few moments,
And share them with your Father above.

So many things were taking place in my new walk with Him, it was overwhelming. And from all of this, I learned the most wonderful lesson of all. -That He truly is my friend and, if I want His best as I walk down life's road, all I have to do is *just ask.*

Just Ask

I'll give you my love if you ask me,
I'll fill your heart until it doth overflow.
I'll give you the peace that you're seeking,
But first I want you to know.

I'll not waste a gift that is so precious,
I'll not cast it just anywhere.
You must know the price that you are paying,
And the weight of the Cross you must bear.

Knowing this, if you seek, you will find me,
The blessings will come without end.
And together we will walk life's pathway,
Together, you and I, hand in hand.

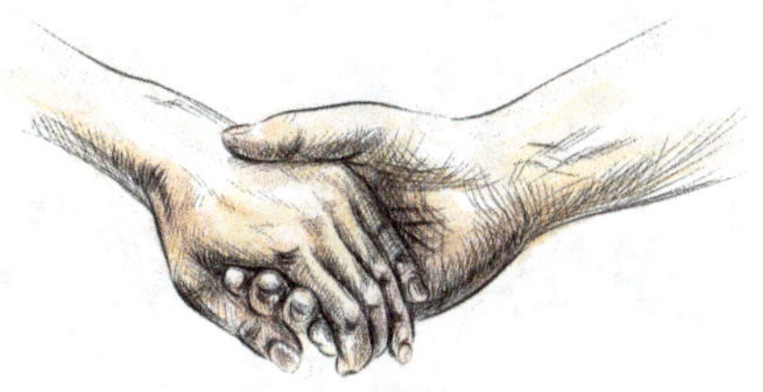

~ Two ~

GROWING UP

Section Contents

This Old House is in Need of Fixing!

This Old House

This old house sure needs a fixing,
So grab the hammer and the nails.
Bring the wheelbarrow and the pick,
Dig out the old paint pails.

Lots of tar paper and some screws,
And lumber by the ton.
Gonna teach you how to build a house,
Gonna have us lots of fun.

We'll make this house look like a palace,
We'll be the talk of the town.
We'll be called the Bridges carpenters,
They'll know us for miles around.

Then we'll sit and admire our work,
Have ourselves a glass of tea.
Yep, we're gonna fix up this old house,
Son, it'll be just you and me.

Then someday, when you are old and gray,
You will thank me for this lesson.
And when you fix up your old house,
You won't have to do much guessin'.

I know right now you are very young,
Play is better than a hammer in your hand.
But there'll be a day you'll thank me, son,
When you become a man.

In the good old days, early in the morning, my aunts and uncles would come to our house to have a big day for slaughtering the pigs and cows. I was always so anxious on the night before all were to come, and I would get up to see if it had snowed. That was so important to me. It just had to snow or it wouldn't be any fun.

They Would Ruin It Every Time

Thanksgiving was a day to remember,
One of the best times of the year.
And always the night before at the window,
I would look to see if the snow was here.

The excitement, I hardly could take it,
As I'd crawl between the sheets for some sleep.
Yes, tomorrow was the day of the slaughter,
We would slaughter the pigs, the cows, and the sheep.

All the aunts and uncles would be coming,
Sometimes there would be a cousin or two.
And we would all be running around like crazy,
With a hundred and one things to do.

It would always start at five in the morning,
First we would make a big spot for the fire.
We would make a big heap with the firewood,
Watch the flames as they leaped higher and higher.

Then we'd get out the old cooking kettles,
And scrub the inside with a stone.
They would have to be clean and spotless,
Most times Mom would do that alone.

The kettles hung over the fire on a tripod,
And were filled full of water with care.
My dad would say, "That's very important,
The water must be hot to remove all the hair."

Next we would set up a couple of long tables,
And lay the knives out neat in a row.
We would get all the hooks and the scrapers,
Making sure everything was ready to go.

My brother would run and get the cattle,
Another would run and get the gun.
If you could have been there to see me,
I would always take off on the run.

But I would come back when it was all over,
I'd watch them cook and render the lard.
Then we would pitch all that was left over,
Out in the old barnyard.

No sooner was it started, then it was over,
Aunts and uncles packing, getting ready to go.
And all that was left was blood, hair, and guts,
All over my nice clean white snow.

I don't remember where this old tabernacle was located, but I do remember going there when I was just a small child, maybe seven or eight years old. It was one of those old-time gatherings of all the *old saints*, as they used to say. People would come for miles around and they would put up the tents, set up the chairs, and throw sawdust all over the place.

There was a waterfall on the campgrounds. Sometimes a few of us kids would sneak out of the service when the shouting got going really good and no one was paying any attention to us. Then we would head for the falls and play in the water.

Maybe they all thought we had just gotten baptized, who knows? Most of the time it was hard to get away unless one faked a pit stop or crawled under the seat because, being the nice little preacher's kids that we were, we all had to sit on the front row. And you can bet it did take up the *whole* row with the size of our clan!

Dad would have us sit there so he could keep an eye on us while he was preaching. One time my sister got out of hand and was acting up. Dad made her go up on the platform and sit facing the congregation for the rest of the service! Poor little thing, I can still see her sitting there with her head bent down staring at the sawdust, and that brings me back to *The Sawdust Trail.*

The Sawdust Trail

My dad was an old-time preacher,
To preach God's word, he did not fail.
Conviction came and people ran,
Down that old sawdust trail.

I'd listen to 'em cry and pray,
They'd pound 'em on the back.
True repentance in those days,
Was something they did not lack.

They didn't care with whom they sat,
Or who was looking all about.
The Spirit came, their hands went up,
And they did sing and shout.

They'd lay their chew right on the bench,
And spread their money out.
I've given all to God, they'd cry,
And there wasn't any doubt.

From the mourners' bench there was a smile,
The burdens were all gone.
They'd jump and run and shout, they did,
And sing about twenty songs.

The sawdust went in whirlwinds,
Sometimes got in my eyes.
But you could tell, no turning back,
No deceitfulness, no more lies.

Today I wonder, it if is the same,
The church so full of pomp and pride.
Among the faking shouts and tears,
Is there something we do hide?

Is the true conviction really gone,
Have we turned as hard as nails?
Maybe we should all just turn around,
And head back for the *Sawdust Trail.*

I was only 10 years old and a preacher's kid... *What did you expect??*

The Old Spider Jar

It's just normal things kids do,
Play jokes on one another.
This time I played it on my sis,
To spare my little brother.
   Like all kids I had my pets,
   Mine happened to be a spider.
   I had to find a real good place,
   Some place where I could hide her.
      So underneath the old car seat,
      With my sis sitting next to me.
      Is where I placed my spider jar,
      About ten inches from her knee.
         Heading for the old campgrounds,
         I slowly unscrewed the lid.
         And released my ol' pet spider,
         I was such a rotten kid.
            Soon he started crawling,
            Right up my sister's thigh.
            Man, she got down right spastic,
            And slapped me in the eye.
               I know you think it's terrible,
               The rotten thing that I had done.
               To me, I was just being normal,
               Just having childhood fun.
                  Sis now has gone on to heaven,
                  And I'm sure has forgive me.
                  That was such a long time ago,
                  Back in nineteen forty-three.

Don't Call Me Names

I'd taken my hard earned money,
And acquired me a nice new BB gun.
I was looking around for something to shoot,
You know, just to have a little fun.

Well, this neighbor kid started poking fun,
And said, "With that thing you couldn't hit a tree."
I pointed my gun right at the boy,
He screamed, "Don't you DARE shoot me!"

And then he ran and made a dive,
In some weeds behind an end line pole.
He started calling me real bad names,
And telling me where to go.

"You say that one more time," I said,
"I promise ya, you've had the course."
Cause I'll pop ya right between the eyes,
And drop ya like a dying horse."

And then he poked his head out,
From behind the old end line pole.
"A beautiful shot," I thought to myself,
"Like an ugly gopher in a hole."

I took a real nice careful aim,
On a spot between his eyes.
And then I pulled the trigger,
Little Sonny Boy, got one big surprise.

He let out a scream and hollered so,
And rolled all over the ground.
My dad came running out of the house,
I stood there shaking, not making a sound.

My dad took my nice new BB gun,
And said, "Come son, come follow me."
For I've something in the barn to show you,
I am sure you will want to see."

I followed my dad into the barn,
And he approached the supporting pole.
Dad took my nice new BB gun,
And put the barrel through a hole.

And then he kind of bent my gun,
Until it looked like a big horseshoe.
"The next time you shoot this thing," he said,
"I'd be careful boy, if I were you."

Doesn't that beat all???
That was the end of my *Red Ryder.*

We had a small farm back in the early 1940's. It was a nice place to have a few cows, chickens, rabbits and some pigs. One night after a prayer meeting, we had arrived home very late and the cows hadn't been milked yet and some other chores hadn't been done. It was one of those pitch black nights where you couldn't see your hand in front of your face, but nevertheless the chores still had to be done. My twin brother and I started out across the field to... I guess you can read for yourself.

Kenny, Keith & Bobby

The Chores Had To Be Done

We had just gotten home from prayer meeting,
And the night was as black as could be.
The pigs hadn't been slopped, the cows not milked,
That was a job for my twin brother and me.

So out across the pasture we wandered,
Calling the cows in the black of the night.
I was so scared I could hardly walk,
My twin was half dead from fright.

We were calling the cows and searching,
Among the tall grass and the weeds.
To take them back to the barnyard,
And then take care of their needs.

We were walking along real careful,
To avoid all the warm steaming spots.
Because the cows weren't feeling the best,
I think most of them had the trots.

All of a sudden my poor twin brother,
Fell right on top of one old cow.
Up she jumped and started running,
How he stayed on, I will never know how.

You could hear him screaming and hollering,
As she raced through the dead of the night.
I stood there frozen unable to move,
It was such a horrendous sight.

My dad and mom came running,
To see just what the matter might be.
Poor twin, he was nigh into convulsion,
Another steaming spot, had been added, *by me.*

There was a neighborhood game that we all used to play. It was called "Andy Andy Over." Don't ask me where that name came from. Who knows, it may have come from me as my middle name is Andrew, and some of the neighborhood kids called me Andy.

Nevertheless, we would take just about any old thing of no value lying around to play our game. One would get on one side of the barn and then one on the other side. We would call out, "Andy Andy Over!" Then we would throw over the barn whatever we had in our hand, as hard as we could. The objective of the game was to see who could catch the most objects coming over the barn without dropping them. You never knew just exactly what your opponent was going to toss over, and it was a dare to see if you had enough intestinal fortitude to catch it or not. "Well brother, I dare you." ...You really did, did you??? *Yes, I really did.*

Okay, okay, that was eighty-some long years ago. I know we don't do things like that today, and besides, my brother caught her anyway!

Andy Andy Over

It's a silly old game, we've all played it,
Most times with a stick or a ball.
And when I was a kid, I did play it,
With something you'd say beats it all.

What a game, it always was a challenge,
To see who would be the first one to miss.
Sometimes I would surprise my opponent,
And I won't blame you, if you don't believe this.

One day I had thrown the ball over,
It seemed it cleared the barn by a mile.
And while my brother was searching and looking,
I looked for something else to throw -*and wow!*

Oh the delight, the thing I had spotted,
But the big decision would be, if that...
Yes, if my brother really would catch it,
I wondered, would he really catch my cat?

It is true, by the tail I did grab her,
She screamed and clawed at the air.
I gave her three swings, she went over,
And then I tore right out of there.

But brother so gently did catch her,
Blood running all over the ground.
I wonder, is he still searching for me,
You can bet, I was no place to be found.

p.s. It was a little cat, and really my brother didn't get scratched
all that bad. Of course, I wouldn't do anything like that today.

It is bound to happen...

Around 1946, my dad was the pastor of the Troy Gospel Tabernacle, located in Troy, Ohio.

One Sunday morning, in the cold of the winter, we had just arrived at church, taken off our coats, and we were standing in the foyer greeting the church members and visitors. My future wife's Aunt Imogene came in from the winter cold, bundled up in her nice warm winter coat. Now Auntie always had a smile and a handshake for everyone. Imogene was one of those friendly, outgoing, sweet-as-could-be, straight-laced, old time Christian ladies. Nothing ever out of place, said or done. You know what I mean? One of those old time saints, prim and proper... *Oh goodness, excuse me did I say prim and proper??? Lord forbid.*

**Mom & Dad Bridges at the old Troy
Gospel Tabernacle**

My Auntie

This story is about my Auntie,
A sweet gal you will agree.
And when she reads this silly poem,
It will be the death of me.

But it really is the truth,
Indeed it is a fact.
It happened on a day in church,
About something she did lack.

Now my Auntie was so proper,
And fixed herself just so.
She really loved the Lord, she did,
And wanted everyone to know.

While standing in the foyer,
Just as sweet as she could be.
She looked so prim and proper,
Like an Auntie ought to be.

She had taken off her winter coat,
And hung it neatly on the rack.
It was obvious, though, to the rest of us,
That there was something she did lack.

My father came right up to her,
And gently took her by the arm.
"Auntie, you'd better come along with me,
Now we don't mean you any harm."

"It isn't that we don't love you -- But you are stirring up a mess.
There's something I need to tell you, Auntie,
You forgot... *your DRESS!*"

We lived in Greenfield, Ohio, and the year was 1939. Modern plumbing was a luxury not everyone possessed in those days. We just happened to be a constituent of that unlucky part of society that was still using outside facilities, made with wooden seats, lap siding, no windows, and one door with a little half moon cut out at the top to let in fresh air.

But in place of two holes, we were the creative gang. We made us a three-holer lid and that was the talk of the town. At that time, there were eleven in our family and you can bet it was a much needed piece of artwork, conveniently hinged on the back with a nice wooden knob for a handle to be raised and lowered as the occasion was called for.

One day, my twin brother and I... oh gosh, this is really bad...*but so help me, it's the truth!*

So Help Me It's The Truth

It was an early Sunday morning,
And the weather was quite hot.
My mother in her own stern way,
Said, "Both of you get on the pot."

So out across the yard we went,
Little though we be.
My twin brother, well that's another thing,
Me, I only had to pee.

Inside this gigantic room we stood,
Not knowing quite what to do.
To sit upon a three-holer,
Or raise a lid or two?

My brother thought that he would try,
To perform this circus act.
And to balance upon a one inch board,
Was a talent he did lack.

Yes, in he went, I kid you not,
And such a sight I could not bear.
He fell right in that stinking pot,
But yet I grinned from ear to ear.

I was in the house in a second flat,
And let out one horrible yell.
One look at me said something's wrong,
My mom could plainly tell.

Well the rest you can imagine,
And the task that lie ahead.
My mom, she pulled my brother out,
My dad wished that he was dead.

They ran for a tub of water,
And dunked him once or twice.
But I'll swear to you, to this very day,
My twin still doesn't smell all that nice!

The Vision

This story was told to me by my father,
It is eerie, but yet it is true.
It happened when we lived in Ohio,
During the war, in nineteen forty-two.

My grandfather and my dad were sitting,
On bales of hay out in the barn.
Talking about the cows and pigs,
And things to be done around the farm.

My grandfather spoke with trepidation,
And said, "Ralph, how can that be?"
Standing before them, was Dad's Uncle Joe,
In a vision for both to see.

Dad said, "My Uncle Joe had passed away,
Some twenty years ago.
And to see a vision of a man who is dead,
Certainly startles a person quite so."

But there always is a reason,
And God always has a plan.
Sometimes He'll do astounding things,
To reach the heart of a man.

Dad said Uncle Joe just stood there,
With an uncanny sort of smile.
My dad sat there in a state of shock,
He told me *for quite a while.*

Then Grandpa spoke and said to Joe,
"Tell me son, what's it like over there?"
Uncle Joe then said to my Grandpa,
Pop, there is nothing here to compare.

Please listen to me, Father,
With what I tell you in awe and fear.
A man truly is a foolish one,
Who doesn't make his peace up here.

My grandpa was a very old man at this time and had lived his life long and hard. He had raised a sizeable family of seventeen children on a large farm and didn't want anything to do with God, the church, or religion. Throughout the long years of Grandpa's life, this would be one of the last things on his mind.

Grandpa had come to live with us for a few years and that was when Grandpa and Dad had seen the vision while sitting in the old barn in Fletcher, Ohio. He didn't stay with us too long after that, as our house wasn't all that large and, at the time, there were ten of us kids still living at home. Paul, Joe, Kenny, Bob, Phillip, Jimmy and I slept upstairs in the largest bedroom in the house. Norma, Carole, and Judy slept in the small bedroom off of the kitchen. If I remember right, there was a small bedroom off of Mom and Dad's room where Grandpa slept. (That was later made into a bathroom in 1947 when Dad and I renovated the old house.) So, as you can see, it was indeed a house full of humanity, thirteen of us, counting Mom, Dad, and Grandpa.

Being overly crowded, Grandpa eventually moved in with my Aunt Ida, who was my dad's oldest sister. We didn't see him too often after that. Grandpa was a rather mean old man, and the grandchildren weren't all that fond of him. We didn't want to be around him unless we had Mom's apron to hide behind.

Grandpa never forgot the vision in the barn. When he was 99 years old and still in rather good health, he had my Aunt Ida call my father to come over to her house, as he wanted to talk with him. Several of us piled into the old family car and went with Dad to see our grandpa. I remember just sitting in my aunt's house on the couch when Dad went into the room where Grandpa was resting. I was about 10 years old at the time and, having memories of the past, I really didn't want to go in and see him.

I don't know how long it was that Dad was in the room with Grandpa but, when he came out, he was grinning from ear to ear and said, "Grandpa wanted to give his heart to God, and make things right with the Lord. He hoped it wasn't too late to do so." Dad told him that that was what God's grace was all about.

Being ten years old, I don't remember what my reactions really were, but I do remember about 45 minutes later, someone went in to talk to Grandpa and he had passed away. The doctor was called and, after going into Grandpa's room, he came out to tell the family Grandpa hadn't been in any pain whatsoever. He simply closed his eyes and went in peace. The doctor said his heart just wore out.

It is astonishing to me how much impact we have on peoples' lives, whether good or bad, while we are going through this short allocated life span. Most of the time we have no concept we are doing so. What a difference it would have been if Grandpa Bridges had been a Christian before he got so old and moved away.

Bob was just two years younger than my twin brother and me...and of course my twin was my equal, so he certainly was out of the picture. My two sisters were just snotty nose kids only four and six years old; I wouldn't dare use them. My two older brothers, Joe and Paul, well to talk them into something like this, you can bet I had more smarts than that. I can tell you right now, that my mom didn't raise two twin dummies and besides, that little brother Bob really did look something like an *astronaut*. Really he did, honestly, just like a little fat astronaut. Well to me he did...maybe like a kid astronaut, anyway.

This is the old barn.

The Einstein of Aeronautics

It was a beautiful day, that I remember,
The sky was as blue as could be.
Birds hovered in flight, in the bright sunshine,
Butterflies fluttered from tree to tree.

The barn looked so high and inviting,
And the straw stack, piled high below.
It was such a wonderful idea I had,
But which brother could I get to go?

I wasn't familiar with aerodynamics,
It was knowledge that I didn't possess.
But with visions of thrills and excitement,
I decided I should give it a test.

In the barn, I found what I needed,
A horse harness, bailing wire, and some twine.
In the house, an old bed sheet full of holes,
The better sheets, I left behind.

Now to create a homemade parachute,
Would take great talent, you will agree.
My siblings all knew I was a genius,
For sure I was destined to be.

An inventor of homemade playthings,
Ideas, way beyond my years.
Some created squeals of laughter,
And some, I do admit, pain and tears.

The parachute was truly a masterpiece,
And was hooked to the harness with care.
Now came the moment for testing, I wondered,
Would my homemade parachute hold air?

Brother Bob, well he looked like an astronaut,
He slipped into the harness with ease.
His face pale white, his clothes soaked with sweat,
And a bad case of buckling at the knees.

With a little persuasion, Bob was airborne,
The sheet bellowed in the warm summer air.
But a fifteen foot drop to the straw pile,
Is a long long drop, my friend, anywhere.

But the old straw pile softened his landing,
Brother Bob wasn't hurt all that much.
For myself, yes, I've given up aerodynamics,
I have decided, I just don't have the touch!

I escaped again -
Bob didn't tell Mom or Dad, and all he got was scraped knees.

~ Three ~

MY FAMILY

Section Contents

Bev and I were married on June the 19th, 1954. You have already read in the first part of this book, several things that happened while I was growing up and about our married life, so I will not be repetitious at this time and get on with *Part Three.*

This section is about some of the things that happened in the last fifty years of our married life. Things about the children growing up and poems written just for those occasions. Did I say the last fifty years? I had better get on with this book or I will never get it finished. It has taken me twenty some years to get this far. I would like to think so, but I really don't have all that much time left...So on with the story and the poems.

Well, since this book is dedicated to my wife, Bev, it only seems right that I start this section introducing you to her. I told you before that she was quite the gal, and that my friend, is true. We'll get to that and all the love I have for her. However, we did have a few funnies along the way that I have to tell you about...

What can I tell you... Bev and I were married just a matter of months, and we decided to get a bowl of little fish.
   - What can I say?! If the wife asks you, *I say give her an answer!*

Ask The Good Doctor

They don't call me the Good Doctor for nothing,
It's frightening the wisdom I possess.
I would always give my wife an answer,
I'd always give her the one I knew best.

Now we had this large bowl of guppies,
They all seemed so contented to be.
But one was much larger than the others,
And this is what my wife said to me.

How many babies can be expected,
From the fat one that's swimming below?
I couldn't believe that I heard that,
How would she expect *me* to know.

But I firmly believe one should answer,
And explain things the best that he can.
Pull it out of the air if you must,
But for heaven's sake, speak up like a man.

So I told her, "Oh yes, you can tell,
It is a secret that I learned long ago.
You place the fat one in a nice clean teaspoon,
Then bend your head way down low."

"Then you listen and count the little heartbeats,
Rather there be thirty, twenty, or ten.
But remember, Dear, if you think you've miscounted,
Then you must start all over again."

My poor wife....Will she ever learn???

A True Friend Indeed

What is a true friend for but to warn,
When something drastic is to be?
You get on the phone and you call her,
And ask, have you heard the news on TV?

They're warning everybody get ready,
They're blowing out the telephone lines.
So you had better get everything covered,
Because the dust will be silty and fine.

My poor wife is all in a dither,
Stewing around, not knowing what to do.
I told her, "Someone is joking with you girls,
They're just playing games on you."

Well there was no way I could convince her,
She said, "My friend wouldn't do that to me."
I said, "You can't really be serious,
Blow out phone lines? -This I gotta see."

My wife left the house for the market,
To teach her a lesson, I must.
I got out the old vacuum sweeper,
And took two handfuls of dust.

So neatly I placed at each receiver,
A pile of dust, right there in plain sight.
Then I sat down to read the newspaper,
Waiting for her to come home that night.

She came home with her arms full of goodies,
And placed them on the counter with care.
Left her shoes at the door, hung her coat on the rack,
And then saw the dust everywhere.

When she spotted the dust in the kitchen,
My office, the bedroom, and the hall.
She squealed with delight, and did call me,
"Just come look, smarty, you think you know it all."

Right then and there I decided,
To let her have her own way.
And when she started telling her story,
I just sat there with nothing to say.

Now, my poor wife started telling her story,
So happy she'd proven me wrong at last.
I'd wink at my friends over her shoulder,
As if to say, *Her condition's from the past.*

Then one day my sister so sweetly,
Said, "Bev, you seriously can't be!
There's no way to blow out phone lines,
He's pulling your leg, can't you see?"

Now if you could only have been there,
And seen that look in utter distress.
Her face turned beat red with embarrassment,
As she sat there in absolute helplessness.

I laughed as she said, "Oh you're awful,
Why did you let me have my own way?"
I said, "Sweetie, if you had only remembered...
Your friend called on *April Fool's Day!*"

My Wife, My Friend

It will not happen every day,
I could find someone so grand.
That I can feel, way deep within,
You really are my friend.

In sorrow and disappointments,
I know you will always be there.
There is no way, however I try,
No other friendship to compare.

You and I will walk life's pathway,
Always hand in hand.
And I will always love you,
Because you are my friend.

Inamorata

I Love You

Inamorata
My Wife

She is like the blossoms in the springtime,
The beauty of the lilies on a thousand hills.
A ray of hope that shines each morning,
My love, my hope, my thrills.

My burdens she willingly carries,
My joys with me she shares.
In my sorrow, her love engulfs me,
With her, all worries are gone, and cares.

I try often, and yet I can't explain it,
How fast the years just fade away.
Eyes grow dim and raven hair,
All of a sudden is silver gray.

Speech has become inarticulate,
Inadvertent I seem to be.
Still I reach in my despair,
And she reaches back to me.

Someday it will all be over,
That is the way it is meant to be.
One of us will stay, the other must go,
What will be left...are only memories.

This was written for our 25th anniversary. We were blessed with almost 60 years of marriage, and these words still ring true...

It's Only Time

You've heard it said a hundred times,
And yet it's really true.
It seems like only yesterday,
I pledged my love to you.

I've wondered where the years have gone,
Where can they really be?
I pray they've been as good for you,
As they have been for me.

Yes, there have been the heartaches,
And there have been the tears.
We both have had our problems,
But all of yesteryear.

I cannot tell the future,
The past just fades away.
I cannot tell what tomorrow brings,
I can only count today.

So that is why I need you,
Always by my side.
I couldn't make it on my own,
Even if I tried.

This poem, I wrote for Bev on her 70th birthday. In my original book of poems, since it was her 70th, I had to place it near the end of the whole book so it wouldn't mess up my page numbers. Thank goodness for technology and my daughter who helped me figure out how to get this put in the right section!

Happy Seventieth

We cannot change the hands of time,
Perpetual though they be.
We cannot bring back yesterday,
And tomorrow we may not see.

One cannot see into the future,
That is only for God above.
So today, on your special day,
We will shower you with our love.

You have been so kind and gentle,
Throughout these many years.
You have enwrapped your family with your grace,
While you have hidden your grief and tears.

Gathered here today, we honor you,
Your family and your friends.
May God grant you so many more,
As this day draws to an end.

Happy Birthday -
We Love You

Another birthday poem as we were getting older...

I Think

Yes today, I think it is your birthday,
I have tried to keep it in my mind.
But it seems that things just seem to settle,
More or less, in my behind.

I know it is a special day,
Even though one day runs into another.
And I do remember you are my wife,
And I'm sure my children's mother.

I am going to make this day real special,
Maybe do something rather neat.
Clean the house, fix the meals,
And maybe even take you out to eat.

But if I should forget to do these things,
You know, I did have good intentions.
If I don't clean the house or fix the meals,
To our kids and friends, we will not mention.

We'll just say we had a great day,
And did what old folks do.
Just sit and stare into space,
And try to remember just who is who.

Happy Birthday - And yes, I do remember who you are, and I
still love you...

Birthdays were always special at the house with our kids. We would get together as much as we could, even after they were grown. We had a tradition where you got to select your birthday meal and whatever kind of birthday cake you wanted. We men drove the girls crazy because we always had Bev make us her *pudding cake*. The girls thought it was boring, but we still love them anyway. (Hee-hee)

Here is a picture we captured of the girls on one of our celebrations. This is the last one where they were all together. We have such fun birthday memories.

Happy Birthday

A birthday is very special,
An indication of time gone by.
We cannot stop the hands of time,
No matter how hard we try.

So we must reap the harvest,
Store memories of the past.
Dwell on the pleasant things of life,
And on the things we know will last.

We'll put away our heartaches,
And dry the falling tears.
Think only of the precious things,
In the coming years.

No matter what God gives us,
We trust it is for our best.
Until we go to be with him,
In our eternal rest.

So may you now enjoy your day,
May you have so many more.
Stay well and always stay happy,
That is what living's for.

Enjoy every day you can,
Love deep within your heart.
That's what binds us all together,
When we are so far apart.

On several acres that we owned, I always left a small area for the boys to work on after they came home from school. As a father, I felt it was in their best interest. I certainly didn't want them to grow up and be counted in the ranks of lazy neighborhood kids. One day, my neighbor came home while my youngest was working on the "weed patch" as they would call it. This is a small conversation my neighbor friend had with him.

Weed or Roses

"What are you doing there, Robb?
It looks like you're having a ball.
Whacking down those ugly, old weeds,
Before they get too big and way too tall."

"Oh, sure," my son said with a grump,
"It's my dad's idea, *not mine.*
He just mows this whole stinking woods,
And then leaves this dumb weed patch behind."

"Now Robb, you are not to grow up and think,
That life is a big bed of roses.
So your dad is doing what is best for you,
Personally, I think it's a great idea he proposes."

"Of course you would think he's doing what's best,
But it does not complete my needs.
For I'll no doubt grow up all angry and warped,
To think life is just a field full of weeds."

There is something special about getting together with your boys and having a nice peaceful hunting day in the woods. Just to enjoy the good things of life - the fresh air and beautiful panorama revealing God's nature in its original setting... Did I say peaceful???

The Hunters

There is something about a hunting trip,
That one does not forget.
The rabbits hide, the squirrels are gone,
And all you get is soaking wet.

Well, Alan, Robb, Stan, and I,
Had decided on this day.
To have ourselves a hunting trip,
Among the fields of hay.

We picked a spot that we all knew,
It was on the Kunze farm.
And the only warning that we had,
Was *Please guys, don't do no harm.*

Oh, we walked and walked and shot our guns,
At gourds and sticks and cans.
We even shot the old chicken house,
Upon the Kunze land.

Alan shot at an old oak tree,
Stan shot old telephone poles.
I just shot my gun into the air,
Robb blew old shoes full of holes.

Now we had walked this long, long day,
And not a sign of life around.
I'm telling you the truth, not a sign of life,
On a hundred acres of Kunze ground.

Now, eight hours of this nonsense,
Was more than I could take.
So we picked a spot among the trees,
To take a nice long break.

It was so quiet and peaceful,
Not a sound was in the air.
And you could have heard a pin drop,
I think, most anywhere.

Alan, he was taking a snooze,
At the base of a walnut tree.
Robb was gazing into space,
And Stan was sitting next to me.

I pointed to an old squirrel nest,
I'm sure abandoned years ago.
And motioned for Stan to be real quiet,
So Robb and Alan wouldn't know.

Then I shot my gun into the nest,
Stan squealed with great delight.
"You got 'em man, you got 'em good,
You hit that squirrel just right!"

What happened next, you won't believe,
But so help me it's the truth.
And I have three good witnesses,
To supply you with all the proof.

Poor Alan jumped a half a foot,
From off the dusty ground.
And Robb's 16-gauge was in air,
Before Stan could even turn around.

You see, in the nest was this big squirrel,
He must've been there all the time.
And when I shot my gun into the nest,
I hit him with that one shot of mine.

But at the time he made his move,
That was his one big mistake.
For World War Three had just begun,
It's more than one old squirrel could take.

That old squirrel didn't have a chance,
I think Stan shot several times.
And Alan emptied out his gun,
I completely lost track of mine.

But Robb, he won out on us all,
For he had his pump gun going.
And when that old squirrel hit the ground,
He died, without ever knowing.

It really wasn't World War Three,
That put a stop to all his play.
It was just *The Hunters,*
...Winding up their day.

The Kunze farm belonged to my sister and brother-in-law, and
we did have permission to hunt on the confines of their property.
And of course, the old chicken house really wasn't hurt all that
bad; just a few stray buckshot, that is all. As for that old squirrel,
what can I tell you? He was gonna die someday anyway.

During the 1970's and 1980's, I owned a construction company in Heath, Ohio. Without a doubt, there were enough things that happened during that time...I could write a complete book just on them alone.

I had my son-in-law working with me during that time and it was an ongoing thing as to who was going to get the dirty jobs. As far as I am concerned, it wasn't the fact that I was the boss, to me it was just...*all in a day's work.*

All In A Day's Work

Okay Stan, run and get the truck,
We've got lots and lots to do.
Today will be a grand old day,
Something special, just for you.

We're going to this remodel job,
We're gonna paint the hall and floors.
Take out windows, pull down lights,
Remove about a dozen doors.

There's something special for you, Stan,
Oh man, I kid you not.
Today we separate the men from boys,
Yes sir, buddy, you remove the stinking pots.

Oh sure, you want me to hug those things,
Take out the bolts and nuts.
Oh yes, I forgot you are the boss,
So I'll just gag out my guts.

Stan, when it comes to carrying them out,
The boss I be or not,
One thing for certain, where you will be,
Is on the low end of the pot.

p.s. Stan, I is da boss. Me no touchin' them things!

My daughter wanted to loose a few pounds, so she came to me and wanted to make a bet. The first thing she should have known, was not to mess with her dad.

She wanted to bet me that, if she could lose so many pounds in so many weeks, then I would agree to... well, you can read it.

*That was 40 long years ago and she is still possessed
with those diabolical molecules.*

The Ballad Of The Fat Gobbler

She came to me with her silly bet,
Thinking for sure it would cost me dear.
"You pay my way to the lake," she said,
"Or I'll wash your car for a year."

Said I, "Be careful of your silly bet,
You could lose this one, I fear.
You're only thinking of your mid-drift,
But the problem's in your rear."

Said she with a huff, "Just take your bet,
I know what I can do.
I'll lose this fat, I know I will,
The call, Dad, is up to you."

Well, I know you tried so very hard,
To lose that gobbie fat.
And knowing you, just like I do,
You didn't eat this or that.

But yet you lost, and that's my gain,
That's just the way life goes.
And you my dear, will wash my car,
Until the snow storms blow.

The moral of this story, my daughter,
Is don't mess with your old dad.
No matter how you try, my dear,
Your outcome will always be sad.

Remember in Part Two, the story about This Old House? ...
Well, now you have the sequel. I learned a lesson well, Dad.
This is my old house.

My Old House

This is my old house,
And it sure needs a fixin'.
Should I start on the outside,
Or begin in the kitchen?

Shall I start with the windows,
Or tear up the floors.
Jerk off the shingles,
Or yank out the doors?

Maybe I'll burn the old barn,
Just to get rid of the mess.
Where should I start?
Well, it's anyone's guess.

Why not start with the deck,
Or pour cement for the drive.
Well, I may as well get started,
What a job, man alive.

But one thing I do know,
I'll be glad when it's done.
It's a lot of hard work,
And not all that much fun.

But I just keep thinking,
It's all for my spouse.
Thanks to you, *Dad*,
She'll have a nice house.

To think, I started learning all of this when I was 12 years old.

It was early in the fall of 1989. I was doing a remodeling job for some friends of mine in the Granville area when, as the old saying goes, *out of the blue* came this beautiful snow storm. It was one of those totally unexpected things that just happens. I gathered up my tools and headed for home. I knew getting anything else accomplished for the rest of the day was out of the question.

When I got to the driveway of our house, this little rose was all that was left of the rose bush. I went into the house and got my camera and took this picture. It was so beautiful, the bright red rose covered with snow. It looked so full of life and yet I knew it was dead. I have always called it, *My Rose.*

My Rose

My rose, but only for a season,
Beauty glows, but only for a reason.
Leaves drop to wither on the ground,
Life is drained, death lies all around.

What is left is still seen when passing by,
What is heard is the moaning and the cry.
But yet her beauty lingers still,
There is no warmth, but yet you feel.

That there is still life, beneath the snow,
I'll have my picture, so I will always know.
That there is still beauty in my rose,
I ask, how long can she hold this pose?

~ Four ~

MY GRANDCHILDREN

;

Section Contents

Every now and then you will be standing near someone and you will hear them say, "This is as good as it gets." What a true statement that is.

Remember when you held the first one in your arms and you sort of whispered to yourself, "Wow! This *is* as good as it gets." Then, months and a few years later, when they tore up the house, dirty diapers changed, toys all tucked away, you bundled them up and kissed them goodbye, and handed them out the door. You had that same thrill seeing the taillights going as you did seeing the headlights coming. And then, again you whispered to yourself, "Whew! This is as good as it gets." But everybody should be blessed with a couple... grandchildren, that is.

Time is but a vapor....

Many times the grandchildren would come to visit and it wouldn't be long before one or more would come and crawl upon my lap and say, "Grandpa, tell me a story." I would make up little stories and tell them in poetry form. (Some of those poems are included throughout this section.) They would sit there and listen, and their little eyes would light up and get so big.

I really do miss those days. It seems only like yesterday. They are all grown and gone now.

They have their own lives to live now, their schooling, their jobs, and their obligations. Maybe someday they will have grandchildren, and perhaps take the time to sit them on their laps and tell them stories or read some of these that I have written for them. If not, they will truly miss out on one of the greatest treasures of life.

To My Grandchildren

May someday, God give to each one of you the same gifts that He has given me. If He sees fit to do so, sit them on your lap, tell them that you love them, tell them about Jesus, make up short stories and slip them candy when mommy isn't looking. Then read to them these little stories from their Great Grandpa.

I love you,
Grandpa Bridges

It's The Same

And then they grew up,
With that smile on their face.
They will soon all be gone,
No one will ever take their place.

They will have their own lives,
Friends, and many places to go.
I won't see them as much,
But I will always know.

When they do come back home,
By the smile on their face.
I am still their Grandpa,
And no one will ever take my place.

These are their stories...

A Bed Time Story

Doggie Woggie and Kitty Witty,
Were playing out in the yard.
Now they were having a real good time,
But playing way too hard.

"Doggie Woggie," said Kitty Witty,
"Stop, let us take a break.
You're wearing me to a frazzle,
Slow down, for heaven's sake."

Kitty Witty said to Doggie Woggie,
"I know what we can do.
Let's play a joke on Ducky Wucky,
We may as well play two."

Now Kitty Witty and Doggie Woggie,
Started through the woods for the pond.
And when they got almost halfway there,
On Doggie Woggie it did dawn.

"What kind of joke we gonna play?"
Said Doggie Woggie, with his nose in the air.
"I'm not going to tell you now," said Kitty Witty,
"I'll tell you when we are there."

Now as they were walking through the woods,
It got real quiet and still.
"What is that?" said Kitty Witty,
Said Doggie Woggie, "There's something on the hill."

"I am so scared," said Kitty Witty,
"I'm as scared as I can be."
"So am I," said Doggie Woggie,
"It's getting dark and I can't see."

Now, when they heard this terrible sound,
Neither one knew what to do.
"Kitty Witty," said Doggie Woggie,
"Are you sure that wasn't you?"

Well, then old Foxy Woxy, laughing,
Came running through the trees.
"Hey don't be scared, it's only me, guys,
I let out a great big sneeze."

"Well, that wasn't very funny,"
Said Kitty Witty with a frown.
"It scared us nearly half to death,
We didn't know anyone was around."

Well, Foxy Woxy started laughing,
It just tickled him so bad.
Doggie Woggie stood there frowning,
Boy, I mean he was really mad.

"Aww, come on you guys," said Foxy Woxy,
"Can't you two even take a joke?"
But it had dawned on them, what they were doing,
Before Foxy Woxy even spoke.

"Foxy Woxy," said Kitty Witty,
"I'm sorry for what we were going to do.
We would have played a joke on Ducky Wucky,
If it hadn't been for you."

"Doggie Woggie," said Kitty Witty,
"Well that's a lesson we sure did learn.
If we play jokes on other folks,
Then we will have to take *our* turn."

So Doggie Woggie and Kitty Witty,
Returned to their own back yard.
"We're going to be really good kids," they said,
"We are both going to try real, real hard."

And they really did.... *The End.*

It was rather amusing. After I had finished telling the grand-children this little story, I said to them, "Now did you learn a lesson from this?"

"See, you are not to play jokes on friends because, if you do, you can never tell if they will like it or not, and they could get mad and you could lose a good friend."

My grandson said,
        "Grandpa, you are a good one to talk."

As the internet saying goes... LOL

An Old Shirt

It's just an old worn shirt, covered with paint,
And to be honest, it has no value at all.
But there is a story about that old shirt,
That happened, when a lad was quite small.

His gramps was wearing that old tattered shirt,
Covered with grease and grime.
Gramps got careless, but did stop the saw,
Just in the nick of time.

Blood and bone was matted in cloth,
To the hospital, a run was a must.
'Wrapped the arm in dirty old rags,
Cared less about the smell and the dust.

The good doctor said, "Man, that's gonna hurt,
Yes sir, Bud, gonna smart for awhile."
But not one bit of pain, did I feel in that arm,
And I bet you do wonder how.

At that time, a little boy was asking his God,
To not let Gramps' arm hurt so bad.
And never a pain, was felt in that arm,
Just because of a wee little lad.

Thank you, Jason, it never hurt one bit, never.
-Gramps

The Bow Legged Frog

Now there once was a frog with bowed legs,
And no one knew why it had to be.
For it certainly was a hindrance to poor Froggy,
Especially when it came to climbing trees.

What a chore it was to play leap frog,
With all the other little frogs in the pond.
And when climbing upon the lily pads,
He had one heck of a time getting on.

And to watch him ride his tricycle,
It was truly the laugh of *Frog Town.*
Frogs came from the other ponds to watch him,
They came from miles and miles around.

It didn't bother little Froggy that they made fun,
And he never got mad or tried to lash out.
Froggy never, never hung his head in shame,
You would never see him get mad, cry or pout.

Froggy knew, deep within his little heart,
There's bound to be other little frogs like me.
And if I carry the brunt of the silly jokes,
They are sure to leave the other frogs be.

Now the moral of this little froggy story,
Be mindful of people, not quite like you.
You never know, when it could be reversed,
And you could end up in their shoes.

Time Passes On, Memories Never Forgotten

My Secret Love

I am not the first to have one,
Nor shall I be the last.
It's a very special secret,
That is hidden in the past.

There are no guilty feelings,
When I set her on my knee.
And yet in your opinion,
There certainly ought to be.

I have no condemnation,
When ere I steal a kiss.
Or when I squeeze her real, real tight,
What joy and oh what bliss.

I like it when she is on my lap,
And I steal a kiss or two.
Now tell me, if you had the chance,
Don't you wish that it was you?

I hope my wife is understanding,
Although I'll not tell all.
And I'll never give her up,
She keeps my life from being dull.

Maybe I should feel guilty,
When she snuggles up to me.
And then again, why should I?
After all, she's only three!

Brandy,

The past few years, I have been watching you go through the complexity and stress that no one should have to go through at your age, and yet you just seem to hang in there and trust your Lord and truly lean on Him for your help and strength. What a testimony for someone your age. Do you realize how many young people would have caved in, given up, and said God you are not fair? Yet your actions and your commitment have confirmed what a worthy person you are to receive the gift I'm giving you.

Always trust your Lord in everything that you do, and I can promise you that He will never let you down. I knew all along what I was going to do and what I was able to do, and it has been a blessing to sit back and watch to see where your strength was. Always remember that as we walk with Him, in order to *purify us*, He will take us through the fire.

[Written to my granddaughter, who lost her husband just weeks after the birth of their daughter, Madison.]

Today Lord

Take me through the fire,
Refine me, this I pray.
Keep my heart pure, Lord,
As I walk with you this day.

Cleanse me for your purpose,
Dredge me from all slime.
Purify me, Father,
Not my will, but thine.

Swathe me in your kindness,
As this day I walk with you.
Keep my heart in focus,
In everything I do.

So when this day is over,
And I lay my head to rest.
I can whisper to you,
Today, I've done my best.

For I will only be remembered,
Not for what I've done or what I say.
But only for the way I've walked,
With you, my Lord, each day.

We are so proud of you in a righteous way,
Love,
Gramps & Gramma

Another bedtime story...

Something Is Missing

Now God had just finished all of His work,
He looked around with great delight.
But something was wrong, and to His angel's He said,
There is something missing, it just doesn't seem right.

I have made this big world, as nice as can be,
With birds in the air and fish in the sea.
I put a sun in the sky, that is plain to see,
But something is missing. What can it be?

I made all the animals, to run on the ground,
Some are so noisy and from others, not a sound.
Some are real pretty, some homely, it's plain to see,
But something is missing. What can it be?

Just look at the flowers and the beautiful trees,
And all of the nectar provided for bees.
It's made to perfection as anyone can see,
But something is missing. What can it be?

Look at the moon, I made just for night,
And look at the stars, how they shine, oh so bright.
Oh yes, see the clouds? They're beautiful to me,
But something is missing. What can it be?

And I remembered the foliage to help make things grow,
I made apples red, so where they are, we would know.
I made the mist, to cover the land and the sea,
But something is missing. What can it be?

I made all the mountains, so tall and so neat,
I made all the rivers that run at my feet.
I made all the insects, so small, some hard to see,
But something is missing. What can it be?

Then God remembered the most important of all,
He hadn't made man yet, to grow big and tall.
He hadn't made a woman, to be by his side,
To be his helpmate, his joy and his pride.

So God took some earth that he had put there,
and made Him a man with skin, bones, and hair.
And then God made a woman as fair as can be,
But still something was missing. What can it be?

God said, "I know what I'll do. I'll make them whole,
I'll give them my breath, my love and my soul."
And then God did that, just for you and for me,
Now nothing was missing, and God was happy as could be.

The End.

Mountain Of Dirt

I know it is just a pile of dirt,
But the mountain looks so tall.
And I am afraid to jump, Grandpa,
I am afraid that I might fall.

You need to learn to trust me, child,
I will catch you in the air.
Just trust your judgment and your grandpa,
Know that I will always be there.

It is just one leap for a little boy,
One great big catch for me.
But when you land, I will hold you tight,
How much closer could we be?

You have grown now, and I am getting old,
I have not the strength I once possessed.
But I will always remember the leap of faith,
Until I am laid to rest.

Love you Chris,
-Grandpa B

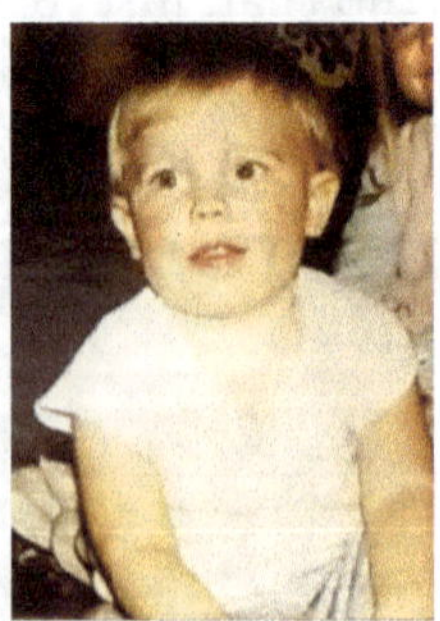

Just a Hound

I know you think I look forlorn,
Sad and ugly as can be.
But way down deep inside, I'm not,
I am as happy as can be.

This is the way God made me,
Really, it doesn't bother me one bit.
So stop your pointing and feeling sorry,
And just get over it.

My Father had a reason,
When He designed me just like this.
So I'll go through life quite happy,
And not too much will I miss.

Be cautious what words are spoken,
Stop and think about what you see.
You are looking at God's image,
Does that surprise you? That God looks just like me!

"Twins"

An Invisible Dot

When we were told there was to be a set of twins in the family, you can imagine what a thrill it was. There hadn't been a set of twins on either side of our family for over 50 years, and that was my twin brother and me, born in 1933.

Sometime in the 1950's, my brother and sister-in-law had a set of twins born, and sadly one of them didn't make it; it is possible neither one of them did. I don't remember the complete story, but I do know ours was the only surviving set to this day. -So you can see, it was a special occasion for us all.

An Invisible Dot

They say there could be millions,
Placed upon the head of a pin.
And one tiny microscopic dot,
Could form a set of twins.

To join a microscopic egg,
Would start conception's plan,
From this union, God had designed,
To form two little men.

To be so very special,
To bring much love and joy.
A gift to cherish always,
These precious little boys.

You can't tell what they are thinking,
By the twinkle in their eyes.
Nor can you tell what they are feeling,
By their moaning and their cries.

They will bring tears and laughter,
As they grow to be young men.
And always they will be to us,
Our special set of twins.

I Am The Worm

Who said I can't be put on chains,
To dangle on your ears?
Or given to your friends as pets,
Or given to your peers?

Don't forget, *I am the worm,*
I can cause you lots of stress.
I can either be your little friend,
Or be your biggest pest.

So look on me with kindness,
And watch the tales you bear.
I well may be a fuzzy worm,
But I can be your worst nightmare.

Doesn't that little green worm,
Look so witty and wise?
With his nose in that book,
And little glasses for his eyes?

He's just a worm nerd,
That certainly is plain to see.
Don't worry about him,
Just you focus on me.

Can't you tell by one look,
And the color you see.
I'm the mean orange worm eater,
That's right...That is me!

I'll eat your stockings,
Your shoes and your dress.
I'll get in your hair,
I'll make you a mess.

I'll hide in your apple,
You'll not know I am there.
Until you take a big bite,
And feel fuzzy orange hair.

Give me to your teacher?
You think you are her pet?
When your teacher sees me,
A bad grade is all you will get.

Hee, hee, I'm just spoofing you,
I am nothing like that.
And my ugly cousin, over there,
Is just blowing smoke out his hat.

We're just cute little critters,
Harmless as can be.
Just destined to be a nuisance,
So don't you worry about me.

Dear Annie

You are such a very special girl,
Winning a portion of my heart.
Your smile, your charm, your sweetness,
Lingers, when we are near or far apart.

There are gifts in life that we receive,
They come from God above.
Some are material, some are temporal,
Some are shrouded in His love.

You are that special gift from Him,
He has placed you in my care.
There isn't a moment of any day,
This responsibility, I fail to bear.

When I have gone the way of man,
And left this world behind.
In times of weakness, in times of pain,
Annie, you will always find.

That I will still be watching,
At heavens portals from above.
I will wrap you Annie, in my arms,
As God covers you with His love.

I love you Annie B,
Grandpa

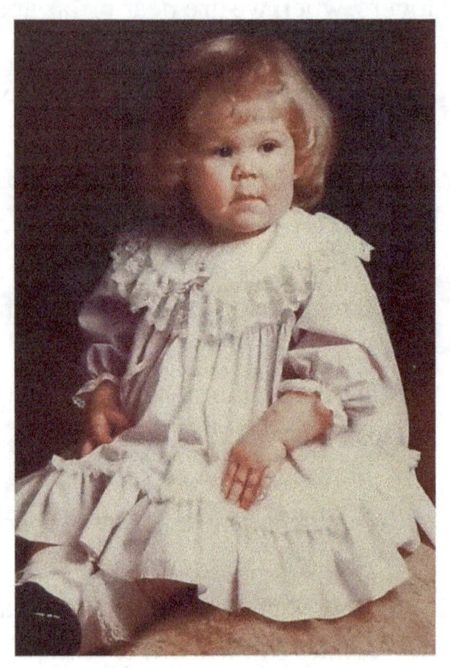

A Porcelain Doll

They are so very fragile,
You handle them with care.
In little ruffled dresses,
With shiny golden hair.

Eyes sparkle like the diamonds,
Skin smooth as new spun silk.
A heart so pure and precious,
And breath of mother's milk.

They're held with such compassion,
You gaze, without a thought.
Eyes join together in silence,
No words, just protection sought.

They're ours, but only for a moment,
It could be years or just a day.
We know we cannot keep them,
The owner will take them away.

They are just on loan to you and me,
So handle them with care.
Remember, they are rare and priceless,
Always keep them in your prayers.

My Christmas Tree

You ask me, what I am thinking,
By my looks you cannot see.
That I am such a happy boy,
Beside my Christmas Tree.

I have my little bear and drum,
I'm as clean as I can be.
You ask me what I am thinking,
Beside my Christmas Tree.

Then we are off to Grandma's house,
A big feast, she will have for me.
And Grandpa will tell me stories,
Beside *his* Christmas Tree.

He'll tell me about a little boy,
One day He was just like me.
How they laid Him in a manger,
Beside His Christmas Tree.

There were little sheep and donkeys,
And the wise men who came to see.
This teeny tiny little boy,
Beside His Christmas Tree.

He will tell me about this special gift,
It was sent from God for me.
That is why I'm having Christmas,
Beside my Christmas Tree.

Now you know why I am smiling, And as happy as can be.
Because I'm such a lucky boy, Beside my Christmas Tree.

Dear Rylee,

It is a time of year when it is just the custom to ask, "What do you want for Christmas? And then the list is made. What a testimony you gave when all you wanted was money to give to the needy and nothing for yourself. That, Rylee, speaks volumes without so many words. We are blessed to have you in our family. Always have a giving heart, and I can promise you, you will have a fulfilled life.

A Giving Heart

Give me a heart like thine, Lord,
A blessing let me always be.
A treasure in your sight, my Father,
A light for all to see.

Give me compassion for those in need,
Let me see their heart and pain.
Then impress on me to do my part,
Not seeking wealth or gain.

A giving heart, is all I ask,
As we celebrate your gift of love.
And watch over me, my Father,
From your habitation from above.

To Rylee, from Grandpa B
Merry Christmas

The youngest granddaughter to join our family was a bit small as my poetry days were slowing down. Putting the final touches on this book, my daughter noticed I'd never had the opportunity to write Avery a special poem. Since I am now a pretty old man, I didn't think I had it in me to write one more but, with a little coaxing, my daughter pulled it out of me. I didn't think it was so great, but she laughed when I came up with the last line, so I guess I'll let her win and keep it in here. At any rate, Avery has always been a good girl and I'm proud to have her call me *Grandpa.*

The Young Lady

There once was a young girl named Avery,
Who grew up to be quite the young lady.
She's lovely and sweet,
She dresses real neat.
And she sure knows how to make *good gravy!*

I Wonder

When I look into this little pond,
You'll not believe just what I see.
Another little kitty cat,
She is looking back at me.

Her fur is my same color,
Her eyes like mine, are green.
I like that little kitty cat,
She's the cutest thing I've ever seen.

She has my personality,
She possesses my charm and wit.
You ask me if it bothers me,
No, it doesn't bother me one bit.

I wonder how long she's been there,
And what she does all day.
How does she entertain herself,
Whenever I go away??

"Margaret"

My Little Friend

I have this little friend of mine,
A joy she is to me.
She really doesn't say that much,
Although noisy she can be.

Like friends, we have our ups and downs,
Sometimes we fuss and fight.
On rare occasions I have spanked her,
Sometimes she hides from fright.

But when the day is over,
Make up, we usually do.
I really like her for my friend,
I think she likes me, too.

One thing about my little friend,
She will do whatever I say.
If I tell her come, she'll come,
If I tell her stay, she'll stay.

At night she sleeps beside me, just lays there like a log.
I know you would like my little friend. My little friend is *my dog.*

In Memory of Mattie

~ Five ~

MY FRIENDS

Section Contents

My Friends

These poems were written about our friends and neighbors. Most of these were written when we lived on top of the hill in Forest Hills in the small town of Heath, Ohio.

This was a great place to raise our children, and for sure there are a lot of good memories to be recorded. If I were to record everything that I would like to, I would be too old to see the keys on the computer to type...so I may as well get on with it.

Dusty and Mary Lou have been our good neighbors and friends for close to forty years. We have enjoyed such good times together and this was on one of those occasions. It was one of those nights that you just didn't feel like going to bed; one of those calm balmy nights that you just wanted to lie out on the grass and look at the stars and marvel at the handiwork of the great architect of the sky.

I was out in the yard with several of the neighborhood kids, having fun and wondering what to do for some excitement. Then it dawned on me, earlier in the day as I was walking along the railroad tracks, I had picked up a rather large clinker and brought it home with me. Now, for those of you who have no idea what a clinker is, it is a piece of burnt out coal that is thrown out from the fire box of a locomotive, a piece of coal that is burnt down to the iron and discarded along the railroad tracks. Well, with my nice large clinker, I decided to play a joke on *my gullible friend...*

Mary Lou Choo chooo choooo.....

My Gullible Friend

The night was calm and balmy,
The stars were shining bright.
I was out running around,
Wondering just what to do that night.

That day, I had been out walking,
Along the railroad tracks.
I had found a railroad clinker,
And gently dropped it in my sack.

So I got the railroad clinker,
And oiled it up just right.
I took my trusty blow torch,
And heated 'til it was shiny bright.

I took it to my neighbor's yard,
And placed it in a selected spot.
I had to be so very careful,
Because it was still real good and hot.

I then got on the telephone,
And gave my friend a ring.
Oh I could hardly wait,
Until she saw that crazy thing.

"Hello," she said, "and who is this?
The hour's late you know."
Said I to her, "You've missed it all,
There's really been a show."

"The meteorites are falling friend,
They're falling far and near.
One may have even hit your yard,
Or hit your house, I fear."

"You're crazy as a lunatic,"
She said in her stern way.
"Now go to bed, I'll take a look,
Not now, some other day."

Well now with much persuasion,
I got her to the door.
And when she saw that clinker,
Oh the look, I could hardly take no more.

Up and down and all around,
She jumped with joyful glee.
"It is, oh yes, it really is!
Oh, Dusty, come and see."

And then the realization hit her,
It hit her like a ton of bricks.
"Doggone you," she said to me,
"That's no way to get your kicks."

And yet that smoldering piece of coal,
Has found a way into her heart.
And I know with my railroad clinker,
My dear friend will never part.

To this very day, it is on her hearth,
It is there, for all to see.
It's a reminder, if they ever move again,
Goodness - Don't move near guys like me!

In spite of the pranks and shenanigans, Marylou and Dusty continued to be our neighbors and dear friends through all of our years. And, as families go, our kids grew up and we continued to enjoy celebrations together. When their oldest daughter got married, we were at the reception sitting near the grandparents, who they called "Pop and Mom". It was a fun celebration and I could tell Pop and Mom wanted to join in... But should they? Did they?? Maybe with a little coaxing from the neighbor friend...

Me and Pop and Mom

We were having this big wedding,
Down in Newark way.
Their Mom & Pop sat near us,
I'll not forget that day.

The ceremony was all over,
And people loosened up a bit.
The kids were all a dancing,
Pop and I were changing wits.

I'd seen both of 'em looking,
At the kids a swinging so.
I said, "You wanna try it?
It really is the go!"

Said I, "On this occasion,
Everybody's gotta try.
Come on, Pop, you can do it,
It's either do or die."

"My old bones, they just won't take it,"
Said Pop, with a long sigh.
"But by golly, I'm gonna do it,
By golly, why not I?"

Pop looked like he had popped a cork,
To watch him dance that jig.
Why I'd put that sly old geezer,
I would put him in any league.

Poor Mom, she was embarrassed,
To watch him acting so.
I told her, "Never mind him,
It's all the rage, you know."

"You want to dance?" I said to her,
With a twinkle in my eye.
"Oh heaven's NO," she said aghast,
"I wouldn't even try."

Well I touched her arm so gently,
And felt her shudder so.
I knew one little tug from me,
On the dance floor she would go.

"Oh we really shouldn't,
It's against the church, you know.
And it really is Peggy's wedding,
So we mustn't steal the show."

Like a cunning sly old fox,
I got Mom on the floor.
Round and round and round we went,
Until we could go no more.

The music took a different pace,
And I kinda held her tight.
Now Mom, she won't admit it,
But she'll not forget that night.

And as I squeezed her softly,
She whispered low to me.
"We really shouldn't act like this,
For all the folks to see."

Well, now I'm getting old myself,
I'm kinda sorry for what I'd done.
But true, we only live just once,
And Mom, it sure was fun.

p.s. If sometime we're together,
And you make sure no one will know.
I'd like to have just one more dance,
Wow Mom, what a way to go.

-Your friend,
Keith

The Nice Guy (*I really am*)

You should all have friends like our neighbors,
　The sweetest family there ever could be.
Now I'll tell you a story that happened,
　When they were living next door to me.

I was in my garage fixing some motors,
　Tinkering around, doing this and that.
And in walked my neighbor's little girl,
　Bundled up in her coat and her hat.

"What are you doing Mr. B?" she asked,
"Oh just working my sweet little friend."
And then her questions started flowing,
And they came and they came without end.

Finally I just couldn't take it,
　I said, "Marcia, that is enough.
I don't mean to sound like the bad guy,
　All mean and grouchy and gruff."

"But you are bugging me while I am working,
It's plain to see that you are getting my goat.
And the only way I know how to stop you,
Is to nail you up by your coat."

I grabbed her and got me a hammer,
And nailed her right there on the wall.
I laughed, because all of a sudden,
Little Marcia was now seven feet tall.

She yelled, she squirmed, and she wiggled,
And said, "I'm telling my mommy on you.
Mr. B you can't treat little girls like this,
You know it's something you shouldn't do."

"My daddy's gonna come and get you,
And you're going right straight to jail.
That'll teach you, to not hang little girls,
Up on the wall with a nail."

Now Marcia, I think you should thank me,
And tell me you think I was fair.
Because if I wasn't so full of compassion,
I promise you - *You would still be there.*

This next poem is about our other good neighbors and dear friends that lived next to us in Forest Hills subdivision. We would get together quite often to play games, and naturally we would reminisce about our families growing up.

We always got the biggest kick out of our friend as she would go on and on about how she had to take care of *all those kids* all by herself because her husband was always at the office and had to work late. Now that wasn't bad enough, if he wasn't at the office working late, then sure enough he was playing tennis with the boys at the club and she had to take care of all those kids by herself. She would say, "I just don't know how I did it."

This was always in great humor with a lot of teasing. This poem was written just for her, and we've had lots of good laughs over it.

I Don't Know How You Did It

I am not surprised your hair is gray,
And wrinkles on your brow.
I don't know how you did it,
I never will know how.

Around your feet all day and night,
All those teeny weeny tots.
Half of them still in diapers,
The rest, half trained on pots.

You'd drag them to the grocery store,
They'd scream and all throw fits.
I don't know how you did it,
You must be out of your wits.

And Sundays, one would have thought,
It was your day of rest.
I don't how how you did it,
With all those little pests.

And when you moved from house to house,
All alone, you did the packing.
I don't know how you did it,
Screaming kids with colds all hacking.

And how you took that camper,
All by your little self.
Packed the bedding and the linen,
Stacked canned goods on the shelf.

Ken, you should hang your head in shame,
The macho man you say you are.
Carol, I don't know how you did it,
All alone in that big car.

Ken, you weren't any help at all,
You never were around.
Just playing tennis and having fun,
While she dragged those kids to town.

Well, I could tell you much, much more,
But time does prohibit such.
And I still don't know how you did it,
You just have that mother's touch.

For the record, this poem was totally in fun. Those kids were, and still are, just as nice as can be. (And so was Ken.)

All of our kids were very well mannered, and we sure did have some funny times....

Please Pass The Cookies

I must tell you a story about Peggy,
One that she will never forget.
I was going to town for some groceries,
Beside me in the truck, Peggy sat.

She felt so big and important,
She held her head high in the air.
Watching the cars and the people,
Not having a worry or care.

In the glove box, she spotted some cookies,
"They're hard," she said, "And not fit to eat."
Now you just don't toss old cookies,
With them, you do something real neat.

So we pitched our Oreo cookies,
In cars with their windows rolled down.
Peggy screamed and giggled with laughter,
Until we were clear out of town.

We arrived home with all of the groceries,
Peggy started home on the run.
As she ran, I'll not forget her last words,
"We gotta do that again, that was a lot of of fun!"

Peggy, I'm saving my old cookies,
Some day, I'm sure you'll be back.
But, we'll be too old then to toss them,
You can just take them home for a snack.

Stay Out

If you have ever played "Forest Hills" Golf Course,
Then you will know what I am talking about.
There is a farmer's field by the Number One tee,
And a sign that reads, "You had better stay out."

One Friday afternoon we had decided,
To have ourselves a nice game of golf.
Now being the nice guy that I am,
I let my friend be the first to tee off.

He approached the ball with perfection,
He placed his feet with much care.
It was a beautiful, beautiful down stroke,
And the ball was aloft in the air.

And then as was to be expected,
It started off in a hook.
"It's going into the farmer's field," I cried,
My friend said, "I can't bear to look."

Well you can't bypass a new Titleist,
You just have to go look for the ball.
And pray that the old farmer is napping,
And not in his field after all.

We headed for the field with caution,
Both looking this way and that.
You could always spot the old farmer,
You could tell by the size of his hat.

Not seeing any sign of the farmer,
My friend stepped across the line.
I let him go in and start looking,
And I lagged just a little behind.

My friend is searching the cornfield,
Just laughing and having a ball.
Not having the slightest idea,
The farmer is hiding and watching it all.

"Come out, Mr. Farmer," I hollered,
"Come out to meet my friend and me.
This is my good friend, Mr. Hocky,
A horrible golfer, as you can plainly see."

Well, with that, up and jumped the old farmer,
His mean trusty dog by his side.
"I'll come out you no good golfers," he said,
"I'll have both of you, I'll have your hide."

Now we weren't meant for the Olympics,
But we broke every record that they had.
Safe in the fairway, we both rested,
Jim said, "Man, it just doesn't pay to be bad."

Now I will add, that this was an ongoing thing with the golfers on this golf course. This guy was determined that no one, and I do mean no one, was going to get their golf ball if it landed in his field. The old farmer would walk the cow pasture daily with his mean old mangy dog and rusty pitch fork that looked like something my grandpa would throw away, just challenging anyone to cross over the boundary line and go into his field.

It was more or less of a game, who could get their ball and get the heck out of that field before the man or the mangy dog got to them. So it wasn't like we were being nasty or anything like that, we were just trying not to get... Let's go to the next story. It is about the same thing as getting *caught in the act*.

Caught In The Act

To see two grown men panic,
Is really more than one can take.
I'm going to relay to you a story,
That happened near Buckeye Lake.

I have this friend named Jim,
Who would help with anything I would say.
And the task that lay before us,
Had to be done in a single day.

We had the trucks and the tractors,
We were doing a really good job.
"What shall I do with the trash?" Jim asked,
I said, "Just pile it there on the knob."

We finished and looked around us,
The job we finished, looked really great.
"Oh no," said Jim, "The trash is still here,
And the hour now is getting late."

"Just pile it on the truck," I said,
"I'll tell you what we can do.
There is an old farmer's field not far from here.
We'll just dump a load or two."

Now at the end of dumping our trash,
Cleaning up and getting ready to go.
This big red truck came screeching in,
I mean, he was coming in flying low.

In a cloud of dust he came to a stop,
And blocked the entrance by the gate.
Poor Jim, he was just plain panicked,
And I threw up everything I ate.

This big husky farmer came running,
With his two old mean vicious dogs.
Jim made a dive for the cab of his truck,
By three feet, I cleared a pile of logs.

"What in the world are you doing?!"
Said the farmer with a vicious grin.
"You're both going to spend the night in jail,
After I turn you in."

Well what does one do when caught in the act,
and you have no place to go?
You just stand there and take it like a man,
And pray the panic doesn't show.

Poor Jim, he tried to answer,
But his lips were quivering so.
And my tongue was stuck to the roof of my mouth,
And sign language, the old farmer didn't know.

"Please mister," I said, "We'll clean it up,"
And with that he flew into a rage.
"How you gonna clean up a bunch of trash," he said,
"When you're both locked up in a cage."

All poor Jim could see, was the headlines,
"The Principal is Caught in The Act."
And I certainly would be the talk of the town,
From the morals that I did lack.

Now if it hadn't been for Jim's little girl,
She was crying and carrying on so.
It must have melted the old farmer's heart,
For he decided to let us go.

"I'll tell ya what I'm gonna do," he said,
"I'm givin' you both a break.
You clean up that mess and get out of here,
And not much time are you gonna take."

Well, time is what we did not need,
It went on faster than it went off.
And we were in our trucks and out of there,
While the farmer's heart was tender and soft.

I can still hear my friend as he whispered,
"Thank you, God, for the blessings you give.
And I'll never dump trash in the farmer's fields,
Ever again, I promise, as long as I live."

Okay, now let me clarify a little bit of this story. It really is true, and just that way it did happen. The farmer's field I am talking about, was about three miles from where we were doing a landscaping job for a client near Buckeye Lake. For years, there had been a lot of people dumping trash there already. Most of the trash was just dirt, old concrete, mostly fills, and things that could be burned. It was an old abandoned farm and had been so for many, many years.

People started dumping waste that would not burn and that old farmer was getting tired of it. He made up his mind that, the next time he caught someone dumping trash on his property, they were without a doubt going to jail.

We did tell him we didn't know we couldn't dump there anymore and were very sorry. With a grump, he said, "It's a good thing you got that little girl with you and she's crying for her daddy – or you would both be in jail. Now get the **** out of here, and I'm following both of you all the way home."

Oh yes, you can bet your bottom dollar, we lost him in the dust. We never saw him again!!!!

p.s. Dumping trash in farmers' fields is a big no-no.

In the fall of '84, I was remodeling a house for a man named John. John came in from the office one night and we were sitting reminiscing about our old Army days. John said, "Keith, I'll tell you something that is so hard to believe... While I was in the service doing my duty for good old Uncle Sam, my friend and I had decided one night to go out on the town. Well, we ran into these two girls walking down the street and started a conversation. Naturally being in uniform, they were attracted to us, so we all hit it off quite well. After about an hour, we all agreed to go to this quiet park to relax for awhile. Now Keith, I was just sitting there and had my arm up on the park bench, lightly on her shoulder and, so help me, it slipped off and my hand just lightly touched her by accident, *an honest to goodness happenstance.* Keith -Up she jumped and her friend with her, and off they went running home!

The next day, I was called into the Commander's office, and he informed me that the girl's father had called the Command Post and said they had better ship me out, as I had *violated* his little girl and, being a Pentecostal preacher, *that sinner boy was going to pay dearly for such diabolical actions."*

Well, John and I had a good laugh over his story. The next day after he left for his office, I took this poem I'd written that night before, and hung it on his bathroom door. He got such a kick out of it, he said, "Keith, you should put that in a book some day." -- My friend, you left this world many years ago, but here is your poem. It's a might risque, but not so bad for this day and age.

Poor John

I will now tell you a funny story,
One that you will probably doubt.
It is a humorous type of story,
And Poor John is what it is all about.

John, now he was a young man,
And had decided on this day.
To don his country's uniform,
Uncle Sam, would have it no other way.

Yes, John he joined the ranks of men,
And indeed became one over night.
Only to find himself one day,
In this awful, awful plight.

See, John he had decided,
On Leave one night, to play.
And he got himself a Pentecostal,
Poor John will not forget *that* day.

John, if there is one thing I need tell you,
Always remember this my friend.
In distress, a Pentecostal girl,
You never, ever lend a hand.

Because if you had stopped to reason,
For yourself, John, what was best.
You'd kept both hand in your pockets,
...And off a Pentecostal's breast.

Sometime in the late 70's, I was involved with the local Jaycee chapter in our area. It was an annual event for the local Jaycees to host "Family Day" around the square in our home town in Newark, Ohio. We would have barbeque chicken, roasted corn, baked beans, and all the trimmings that go with our annual event. There were street games and rides for families and their children, with nice shaded areas for the elderly to sit on park benches and watch the activities.

On this one occasion, we were in dire need of a large kettle for hot water to prepare the corn on the cob. One of the men working with me said, "Where in the world would we ever get a kettle that big?" I said, "Don't worry about it, I will go and retrieve one from my friend, Skip. He will be glad to lend us one from his restaurant."

... As Paul Harvey would say, *and now for the rest of the story.*

They'll Do It Every Time

Hey Skip, old buddy,
Old pal, old friend.
I need a kettle,
Would you lend me a hand?

We're having this shindig,
Down Newark way.
And I need me a kettle,
Need it just for one day.

Why sure, Keith, old pal,
Stay right where you are.
I'll lend you a kettle,
I'll even bring it down in my car.

But one thing I ask,
Is please when you are done.
Will you please bring it back,
Because I have only one.

Hey, no problem old buddy,
Consideration I don't lack.
When I am done with that thing,
I'll bring it right back.

Yes sir, old buddy,
Don't you worry at all.
One thing I don't need,
Is a kettle that tall.

Skip, after thirty-eight long years,
Your old kettle's gotten dull.
But I want to bring it back to you,
Crud, rust, and all.

Now all that I ask, Skip,
Is when I dine in your place.
Don't make my soup in this kettle,
Use it in some other place.

You have been a good buddy,
Gone through lots of grievin'.
But I'm seventy now, Skip,
Let's not try to get even.

Let's drop the whole matter,
And shake hands on the deal.
You just sit back and relax,
And keep popping your pill.

Life's way too short, Skip,
To get all excited now.
I'd make it up to you, buddy,
But I just don't know how.

p.s. Skip, I really do have that thing,
Like I said, crud, rust, and all.
And if you really do want it back,
Just give me a call.

There was a restaurant near our home town that we patronized quite often. They were noted for their home cooked meals and excellent taste. One of the main reasons I liked to go there was because I knew they had real homemade mashed potatoes, not the instant kind that I personally cannot tolerate.

One night, as we sat down to eat our meal, I took a bite of potatoes and said, "Can you believe this? These potatoes are not real. They have started to use instant potatoes in this restaurant. It doesn't matter what the rest of you say, these things are not home-made mashed potatoes.

After several others tasted theirs, the conclusion was that I was totally insane, and the potatoes were as real as real could be. I called the waitress over to explain the situation and voice my opinion of using instant potatoes, and she said, "Sir, we never, never, and I mean never serve anything but real mashed potatoes here at this restaurant. Everybody knows that. That is just something we would never do." I said, "Well, sorry, but I can tell the difference, and these are not real."

Naturally, was all done in a joking way and the gang got a big kick out of proving me wrong. Welll, they *thought* so anyway. These two poems I wrote and sent to the restaurant the next day.

Welcome To Clark's

We are not perfect but we try.

There just isn't any place in town,
You find a spot so grandiose to eat.
Where we will smile and humbly bow,
And do service at your feet.

We spread our table's just for you,
We will treat you like a king.
We'll feed you until your tummy's full,
Just ask, we'll give you anything.

Our peas and beans are garden fresh,
Our chicken is so superb.
Our potatoes, you can bet they're real,
We give to you our word.

But, if we should get into a bind,
And see our stock is running low.
We have just one, sample of spuds,
Now tell me who would really know?

But to be very honest with you,
It did happen, once, to a man in Heath.
We don't even know who it was,
Someone told us his name is Keith.

Our waitress came out later and said, "You won't believe this, but we just ran out of potatoes! The cook had us hand him that box of instant spuds a salesman left the other day. He said no one will ever know the difference. Then he saw you taste yours and said, "Oh no, we got caught. That man knows they're not real." – Nevertheless, we all got a good laugh.

We Are The Cooks

There are some things we do not do,
If we are to keep our word.
We do not serve a frozen pie,
And wouldn't, if we could.

We would never take a Wonder bun,
And set it before our guest.
For after all, most of them,
Really do know what tastes best.

We do not take our peas and corn,
Out of a Kroger can.
And remember all of our salads,
Must be tossed by hand.

We never brew the coffee,
Until it is black and strong.
We never use a cheaper grade,
We know that that is wrong.

We do not take our problems,
To a table that we have spread.
We know there are so many things,
That are better left unsaid.

The chicken must be fried just right,
For the word is out around the town.
Not too soggy, not too light,
It must be juicy and crispy brown.

And we never, never serve instant spuds; that is a cardinal sin.
For there is bound to be one guy, who'll be back and turn us in.

There is nothing like a good old camping trip down by the lake side. And then again, there is nothing like a good old camping trip down by the lake side with your best dingbat friends. -Our trip was taken in 1979 near Zanesville, Ohio.

The Dillon Gang

I've written poems for several occasions,
Some humorous, some deeper in thought.
This one is a real classic,
You'll like it, I think, well you ought.

It's about a camping trip at Lake Dillon,
Our friends from three states were there.
The sight we picked, well, was something else,
No trees, lots of bugs, and foul fishy air.

We got out of the cars and looked around us,
No grass, tall thistles and lots of weeds.
A dilapidated old out house nearby,
To meet our everyday needs.

The girls fussed because of no water,
To carry it a mile, we men agreed, they must.
Don't gripe and complain, you poor ladies,
It's just down the trail in the dust.

Then John, Larry, Eddie and I,
Proceeded to put up the tent and the junk.
It's good, we four fellows went with them,
At least there were four with some spunk.

Ten minutes in the operation, Mother Sondra,
Grabs the broom and starts beating the air.
Sharon picks her teeth with the only meat fork,
JoAnn sat and blew smoke in our hair.

Thank goodness, one day's down, and it's nighttime,
And we all sit around the campfire.
Too lethargic to talk, just staring,
Watching flames, shoot higher and higher.

After the debating and stories were all finished,
To get some sleep, Sondra said that she might.
Sharon got up and tripped over the campfire,
JoAnn screamed and hollered with fright.

Among the musty sheets, I finally nested,
While Bev placed her feet on the shelf.
John grinned and muffled a laughter,
So did JoAnn in spite of herself.

At three in the morning, I'm all smothered,
I awoke, Bev stumbled; fell sitting on my head.
And by then, my mouth is so raunchy,
I think to myself, I'm half dead.

"What's going on?" said Mother Sondra,
"Get up," said Ed, "Give the poor guy some air."
"Well, I gotta go real bad," cried Beverly,
And it's dark and creepy out there.

At three in the morning, it's all out for pit stop,
The girls giggling and dancing about.
Larry slams his head into his pillow,
To make it through the night, I had my doubts.

It was up bright and early for breakfast,
The smell of bacon and eggs filled the air.
And the glorious sight that did greet us,
No make-up, no teeth, messed up hair.

As soon as it started, it seemed over,
Tearing down and getting ready to go.
Yes, we still laugh and talk about it,
That was nineteen long years ago.

I had my doubts about putting this poem in my book. I thought maybe it was too long and too much of a story. But after reading it again, I decided to go ahead and add it. You can stop any time and skip it. I will never know anyway.

Our church wanted to have a special dinner for all the ones who worked on the bus route to show them our appreciation for the many hours they put in each week to organize, pick up, deliver, and handle about 50 to 60 kids from all over town.

Bev and I had Junior Church for them after they were dropped off at the main entrance. We kept them entertained with a prepared program, Kool-Aid, and cookies for well over 45 minutes. Oh yes, it was time to send them back home.

This is about... The Bus Route.

The Bus Route

On this special occasion, I wrote a poem,
About all of you, who work on the bus.
I really didn't know just what to write,
But I was asked, so I figured I must.

There isn't that much about all of you,
That really has come my way.
And to write a poem, that would do you justice,
Would take up about half of my day.

I thought about Dave driving the bus,
And getting stopped for speeding around.
But someone has to pick up those kids,
And bring them halfway across town.

I think of Mike as the quiet guy,
He just grins and doesn't say much.
When you watch him with the tough kids,
You know for sure, he hasn't lost his touch.

And Molly, with her little yellow junker,
They can tell when she's coming around.
She's considerate when she coasts up to the house,
Just to keep the muffler noise down.

Poor Andy, every bus route needs a farmer,
Without one, now tell me how would one do?
You need someone to wipe that dirty little nose,
Clean up the mess, the trash, and the goo.

Dallas, how do you keep those buses running,
With a pipe wrench, some wire, and a jack?
But I'll say the job you do must suit them,
For I notice they just keep bringing them back.

I was sure married life would ruin Lani,
And the bus route would just have to go.
But she's hanging in there like a tough gal,
Just praying the wear and tear doesn't show.

I'd like to thank Tom, for giving his service,
It is a huge sacrifice we all will agree.
I am so grateful for the day you came along,
If you hadn't it would probably been me.

Earl, truly has been the organizer,
Running around, getting everything done.
Doing his best, to keep everyone happy,
Trying to convince us, it is a whole lot of fun.

There are the cooks, babysitters, and the fill-ins,
I am sure, everyone doing your part.
Giving the most of your time and your talent,
But most of all, giving from your heart.

There are, no doubt, many more of you,
I just couldn't name you all one-by-one.
We all know your heart is in the bus route,
You never leave until your day's work is done.

But the thing that I think is most important,
Is to remember why you are doing all of this.
And the times that you think it isn't worth it,
If you quit, think of the blessings you will miss.

Think of the kids and their future,
If it weren't for you, what would it be?
When they bow before God in judgment,
Because of you, that is their eternity.

God has given you a great commission,
It is a commandment, you'll find in His word.
"Bring unto me all the little children,"
I know you would do more if you could.

Remember God is always watching,
He knows when things seem all up hill.
He knows just why you are helping,
If it is half-hearted or because it's His will.

I challenge you, who work on the bus route,
To give it all, and the best that you can.
When you think, you no longer can take it,
Cheer up, God is there to lend you a hand.

~ Six ~

MUSICAL ART PROGRAMS

Section Contents

In the early 1980's, we held *Musical Art Programs* for churches around Ohio and surrounding states. I would load our van with speakers, sound equipment, cables, easel, oil paints, art boards, lights, and everything that goes with a Music Art Program. My family provided music and singing, while I painted an oil painting. During the service, there would be pauses for scripture and reading.

The poems in this section were written for these programs. There were times I would write some of the poems at the last minute. I might feel there were things needed to make the program more complete so, while the kids were going over the music, I would write. It's strange how it always seemed to fit in so perfectly. But that really is the way God works, is it not?

Bev and I would pile in the van (and an extra car) with Michelle, Stan, Jason, Brandy, Robb, Karen, and the twins, and off we would go to the various churches. It would make a long day, but another fun day. By the time we got there, set up the equipment, held the program, took everything down, and loaded it back into the van. You can imagine, it was a long day!

I remember one Sunday, we were in Piqua, Ohio at the Baptist Church. After the service, we had packed everything into the van and went back into the church, as someone wanted to give us a tour of their facility. We could have been in the church a good 30-45 minutes before going back out. I opened the van side door to let the twins in and I smelled smoke. I didn't see any smoke but knew something was burning. I opened the back door of the van and there was the paper sack where I had put the clean-up rags and paper towels that I had used to wipe the oils off the brushes. –The chemical reaction with the oil and paint thinner had started a fire in the sack of trash I stored in the back with the equipment! ...A few more moments in the church and it would have been a long walk home!

The Stone From The Mountain

This program, *The Stone from the Mountain*, we did so many times, I was running out of ways to paint the picture. Once I had invitations to go back to the same church three times to do the same program. The last time, the coordinator called me for this church and I told her, "I just don't have anything new to add to the program." She laughed and said, "Well, the people said just do the same one again!"

Those programs were so rewarding. Great times with family, packing up, loading, tearing down. So much work but well worth it. The *Stone From The Mountain* was the first program we did together.

Between 1983 and 1985, we held the musical art program for close to 20 church services. A short time later, Michelle and Stan, with Brandy and Jason, moved to Colorado. After they moved, I did the programs by myself for several years, and then it just became too much to do by oneself. So, as the old farmer would say, "I hung up the shingle" and just went to writing our events in poems.

For this program, *The Stone From The Mountain*, I would paint in oils on a 24 x 48 inch hard surface art board and then, throughout the service, the kids would sing songs that would correspond with the poems and the painting. It has been a long time ago, and I really do miss those days.

I have included some of the paintings in this section of the book. These paintings would take, on average, about 45 minutes to complete. I hope you enjoy both the paintings and the poems.

The Stone From The Mountain

Oil Painting by Keith Bridges

The Stone From The Mountain

"What are you doing sir, with that little stone?"
Said the lad to the old man as he leaned on his cane.
"Oh, it's just part of my worldly possessions, my son,
Just part of the things in life that I have gained."

"But it's just a stupid stone," laughed the lad,
"Not one bit of good it will ever do."
"No," said the old man, "Come here my son,
I've a story I want to share with you."

You see lad, one day I was just walking along,
And I was tired and hungry and sad.
Now, if I just had a friend or something to eat,
I thought to myself, then maybe things wouldn't seem so bad.

Then from that mountain over yonder, son,
This little stone came rolling down.
I picked it up and held it tight in my hand,
It seemed like a new friend I had just found.

And then I too laughed, son, and said to myself,
It's just a dumb little rock.
And then I was reminded, it was something God made,
It wasn't to be laughed at or mocked.

So, I just slipped it deep into my pocket with care,
And started on my journey with a certain sense of pride.
Always to be reminded, when hungry or lonely,
That I'd always have part of Him by my side.

It's been like a companion these many long years,
I always have it with me, when I sleep or I dine.
Son, I've been beaten and robbed of all earthly goods,
But this little old stone, they always leave behind.

So, you see lad, it's not just a dumb stone,
It's a constant reminder of God's love for me.
It represents the stone that came rolling from Babylon,
The stone that all kingdoms will bow the knee.

My son, one day a stone was cast from the mountain,
To many it was useless, as useless as could be.
By some it was stepped on, rejected and forgotten,
But it was cast there for you and for me.

And I've built my hope on that stone from the mountain,
Throughout life it's been a source of strength for me.
Many times I've wondered what I would do without it,
And this little stone is always a reminder to me.

The little lad gazed at the old man on the cane,
As he shuffled to leave him with a sigh.
He reached for the scarred, wrinkled, bony old hand,
As misty tears fell on his cheek from his eye.

The Rock

The artist stared at the rock for a moment,
His chisel was poised in the air.
His wrinkled brow in deep concentration,
Shall I start here or shall I start there?

I must remember, just one slip of the chisel,
Then all my labor will be for naught.
A beautiful sculpture I will create,
Just from an old piece of rock.

But I am the master, I must remember,
To always have everything in control.
A work of art it will be when finished,
I will put in it my heart and my soul.

The hammer slammed on the chisel,
And the chips piled high on the floor.
The artist worked with great consternation,
As no artist had ever worked before.

Ah, it is finished, he sighed with contentment,
For my King, a perfect piece I present.
And truly, it is in His likeness,
And worth every hour that I spent.

-And I say also unto thee, that thou art Peter,
And upon this rock I will build my church. -Matt 16:18

The Stone From The Mountain

Each of the landscape paintings had slight variations.
Oil Painting by Keith Bridges

Exodus 20:1-18

He paused in thought, as he gazed at the mountain,
His gray hair blowing in the breeze.
What is your will, God? What is your command?
I seek your will, Lord, on bended knees.

Go to the mountain and tarry there, son,
Seek me with your soul and your might.
On a stone from the mountain, I'll reveal my thoughts,
So men will always know what is right.

With my finger I'll engrave what is to be in men's heart,
On a stone from the mountain, I'll write.
It will be my commandments for men everywhere,
To guide them each day and each night.

On a stone from the mountain, I'll devise a great plan,
To lead men back to God's throne.
On a stone from the mountain, I'll teach them my love,
And never again will men be alone.

I'll comfort and lead them, and dwell in their hearts,
I'll wrap them in my arms of love.
In sorrow I'll hold them, in sickness I'll heal them,
As I keep watch over them from above.

The Stone From The Mountain

Oil Painting by Keith Bridges

My Ship At Sea

Even though my favorite program was *The Stone From The Mountain*, I always enjoyed doing the program, *My Ship At Sea*. There was something very special about this program. It seemed to speak to me in so many ways, and you could always sense that it had a certain effect on the audience. I would clean up the brushes, take down the speakers, wrap up the cables, pack the rest of the paraphernalia, get the family in the van, and leave the church and congregation behind us knowing we had touched someone's life. It was such a good feeling.

My Ship

I'll not escape the storms of life,
That is just the way it will be.
It's an awesome responsibility I have,
That God has given me.

To build my ship and build it strong,
To withstand the tempter's gale.
To take the storms at their very worst,
To take them, to take them well.

I'll not falter when the storms come in,
Nor weaken when the billows roll.
My captain then will take the helm,
I will give Him full control.

I may never know what lies ahead,
In life, that is the way it will be.
I just want Him proud, to be my Captain,
When I am out at sea.

My Ship At Sea

Oil Painting by Keith Bridges

Self Portrait

I was like the ship,
Tossed about on the sea.
Being exactly what Satan,
Wanted me to be.

I cared not for the future,
Thought less of the past.
Considering only myself,
And the things thought to last.

I thought the thrills of the world,
Were the price I would pay.
Not caring, although knowing,
There would be judgment day.

And then one day, Jesus,
So sweetly came by.
And said that's enough,
My way, won't you try?

For a moment I panicked,
And backed off in fear.
I was counting the cost,
Knowing the price would be dear.

And yet there He lingered,
And just seemed to say.
You know in your heart,
There is no other way.

Then I yielded my life,
My body and soul.
I laid all at His feet,
And gave Him full control.

And oh, what a difference,
I can hardly express.
The peace that He gives me,
That wonderful rest.

Now you know why the difference,
And the change that you see.
The Ship in distress,
Was a portrait of me.

Worthy Of Its Price

"She is a good ship," said the builder,
I built her well, to sail the seven seas.
She'll take the storms, when at their worst,
However fearful they may be.

"But the price is a bit high," said the Captain,
"A mite more than I can pay.
If you lower the price, a couple of pounds,
I'll buy this ship, sir, I'll buy this ship today."

"No," said the builder, "for I have set my price,
It's a fair one, my lord, you will agree.
I'd buy this ship, if I were you,
Yes sir, I'd buy it if it were me."

Well, the price was paid for the builder's ship,
A handshake and a parting of ways.
The Captain would know if it was worth its price,
He would know in a matter of days.

The ship was launched at the beaten wharf,
The Captain and the crew were all there.
Shouts rang out, as she slid down the barnacle ramps,
And great excitement filled the chilly air.

The ship was loaded with goods from abroad,
Some goods to be shipped down the coast.
The crew with their gear all stepped aboard,
And the Captain with all of his host.

The sails were raised to catch the autumn winds,
The ship was turned toward the open sea.
On her maiden voyage to foreign lands,
Not knowing her destiny.

It now had been many days at sea,
And a tempest began to blow.
The Captain knew at a glance, there was trouble ahead,
There are some things that a Captain just knows.

The salty waves lashed over the ship,
The deck hands took shelter below.
"Will she take the storm?" asked the first mate,
"I don't know," said the Captain, "I really don't know."

"Overboard mates, with all of the cargo!"
Came the orders below from the hold.
"Everything overboard, I say me lads,
Everything including the silver and the gold."

The waves and the rocks lashed out at the ship,
The planking was ripped from the stern.
The sails were battered and torn by the winds,
The huge mast nearly overturned.

The storm subsided, and a calm settled in,
The Captain walked to the port side.
He took the helm in his shaking hands,
On his face was a look of pride.

The first mate stood there beside him,
And watched the sun dance across the sea.
He surveyed the damage across the decks,
"To take a storm like this, what a ship she must be."

"She did take the storm well, my Captain,
Even though at such a sacrifice.
She's a beautiful ship, she certainly is, sir,
And well worth the builder's price."

My Ship At Sea

Oil Painting by Keith Bridges

The Lighthouse

In the art programs I called, *The Lighthouse* and *My Ship at Sea*, I used the same setting on the canvas but all the music and the poems were different.

The message is the same, whether you need a light to guide you or a Captain to take the helm. It is a decision we will all some day come to grips with. Every one of us, young or old, short or tall, skinny or fat, rich or poor, it doesn't matter, you can mark it down in your little book, you and I will make that choice.

Oil Painting by Keith Bridges

The Lighthouse

The storm was at its fullest gale,
It was almost more than the old ship could bear.
The waves were tossing to and fro; Darkness... was everywhere.

The crew had given up all hope,
And in silence, stared into space.
The Captain stood with a ghastly look,
Upon his bearded face.

A young sailor on a barrel sat,
A tear dropped to his cheek.
He was thinking what he had said to his little girl,
"Aww don't you cry; I'll be back in a matter of weeks."

An old, old deckhand held tight to the ropes,
And he closed his eyes in fear.
He'd never been in a storm like this,
Well, not for many a year.

The first mate looked at his sextant,
His voice was husky and low.
You once stilled a storm like this Lord,
It was many many long years ago.

And then in the distance, a light oh so faint,
Yet it could be seen by all the men.
And they knew there was hope from the light on the hill,
For it would guide the old ship in.

A shout went up from the weary crew; They sang in joyful glee.
The Captain just smiled and thought to himself,
If it wasn't for the Lighthouse, where would this old ship be?

The Lighthouse

Oil Painting by Keith Bridges

God's Lighthouse

Oh, how I need God's lighthouse,
To light the way for me.
I cannot make it on my own,
Upon life's troubled sea.

The storms will come and they will pass,
And I will still be there.
But the light that shines from heaven,
That's what will guide me everywhere.

There will be times that I will grip life's rope,
I will close my eyes in fear.
And when the doubts are *if I will make it*,
As His child, I will know that He is here.

Sometimes from human error,
His light I may not see.
But somewhere in the distance,
That hope still shines for me.

I am so glad I have God's lighthouse,
To guide me upon life's raging sea.
And when in troubled waters,
I know where God will be.

He will be right there beside me,
To take the helm in His mighty hand.
Against the storms oppressing,
Together we shall stand.

I'll See You In The Rapture

There were only two times we did the program called, *I'll See You In The Rapture*. This program was fun to do, but it was very difficult. To try to paint a picture of Heaven and to really do it any justice is beyond human comprehension. And besides that, who in the world could even begin to compete with God?

I don't have a painting from this program, as I left it at the last church where this painting was done. Here are a couple poems that were written for this program. One of the songs that Michelle and Stan sang for this program was, *I'll See You in the Rapture.*"

It Is My Father's Will

His majesty was sitting on his kingly throne,
And the courts were in full array.
Trumpets were sounded, loyal subjects had gathered,
None attending would forget this day.

But the King was disheartened, it was plain to see,
A great decision had to be made.
And yet, he knew there was only one choice,
On his only Son, the burden must be laid.

"Summons my Son," he announced to his scribe,
"My plans with him, I will discuss."
"But sire," said the scribe, "is he willing to go?"
"Yes," said the King, "he will know that he must."

The Son was brought before His Majesty,
Before his King, he stood straight and tall.
"I am here at your command, what is it you wish?
Whatever you say, sire, I'll do it all."

With misty eyes, the King looked at his Son,
His words were feeble and low.
"I want you to know, Son, it hurts more than you know,
But you are the only one I have who can go."

"Do you remember way back, when you and I had a plan,
And then how it seemed oh so right?
Well, I have received word that it didn't work out,
And oh, how we had hoped that it might."

"So now you must go to that foreign land,
Take this scroll and tell them, thus saith the King.
Bring ye your burdens, bring ye your woes,
Yea, to the Son, ye must bring everything."

The Son kissed his father and bid Him farewell,
With his court, they left for their journey alone.
With a heavy heart and a burden to bear,
The weary King returned to his throne.

"Sire," said the scribe, "it is plain to see,
That something doth trouble you so.
Your Son will return, and even I could tell,
That he was more than willing to go."

"No," said the King, "I know in my heart,
Rejected and beaten he will be.
They will spit in his face and nail him to a cross,
For all the other kingdoms to see."

"But if that is what it takes to fulfill my plan,
Then my Son I must be willing to give.
And yet, my scribe, who knows by what I decree,
How many others will live."

A Special Journey

I would like to take you on a journey,
One that I hope you will not forget.
It is a different type of journey,
Filled with excitement. but only for the elect.

It is a short trip that we are taking,
You see, it happens in a moment of time.
And what a wonderful sight there awaits you,
Where the beauty of heaven does shine.

You arrive at the gate, it is quite awesome,
A city so big and foursquare.
Angels in shining white robes await you,
For you, the Father has them waiting there.

They smile with a smile of contentment,
One reaches and takes you by the hand.
There is a sound, you cannot describe it,
All in harmony, a ten thousand piece band.

The angels in a mighty chorus are singing,
"Worthy, oh worthy is the Lamb."
Tears of joy fill your eyes; you hum softly,
"Redeemed by the blood, Lord I am."

You walk up the streets of pure gold,
The river of life is running close by.
Souls in white robes, doing God's bidding,
No heartaches, no sadness, not a sigh.

You approach the courtyard of God's kingdom,
Behold the Father, the Holy Spirit, and the Son.
You can tell at a glance, they are all well pleased,
They know of the battle you have won.

Everything is ready for your arrival,
In the chamber, all things are in place.
A scribe hands a book to the Father,
The Son has a smile on his face.

For He knows that He will submit you,
And He is not worried one bit, you see.
He knows how often you've spoken His name,
And told others all about Calvary.

He knows how many good deeds are recorded,
And he knows how many hours of prayer.
He knows all about the secret closet,
And how many times you have met Him there.

Of your giving, yes, it is all recorded,
At times where you gave more than your share.
The burdens of friends that you carried,
He knows all the ones you did bear.

Page after page has been recorded,
The angels all smile with delight.
They know for you, a gold crown is ready,
And a beautiful robe of pure white.

The books are closed, the Father greets you,
Welcome my child, well done.
Come, share the joys of my kingdom,
Come, share in them with my Son.

White As Snow

White As Snow was often done in the wintertime because it just seemed to fit. At times, there would be a hush over the congregation with people wiping their eyes, and they would leave their seats to come down to the front and quietly pray.

– I really do miss those days.

Oil Painting by Keith Bridges

White as Snow

Though I try to comprehend it,
I will never understand.
How a Spirit that lives forever,
One day became a man.

How there can be three in Heaven,
And yet One here on earth.
How a girl that never knew a man,
Could give a virgin birth.

I will never understand, how a Spirit,
Who roams the land and sea.
And all the while He is doing it,
He lives inside of me.

I doubt, if I will ever understand,
Why a man is born with sin.
And how it takes the Holy Spirit,
To cleanse his heart within.

I will never understand the greed,
That possesses the human heart,
How it only seems to linger,
When we try so hard to do our part.

Although I don't understand it,
There is one thing that I know.
Though my sins were once as scarlet,
He has washed them white as snow.

~ Seven ~

REFLECTIONS IN SCRIPTURE

Section Contents

It will be quite clear to all of us, the last three sections of this book do not come from any intellectual elite. These just happen to be some poems that I have had in a notebook for years and thought I would include them in my book. In Part Nine, I will end with more lighthearted poems. This particular section is more reflective on things we read in scripture. I hope you enjoy and I hope they leave you with some things to think about.

Before we get into the poems, though, I have to explain that I did try something new once upon a time. Here's how it happened...

One Sunday morning, we had arrived at one of the churches that had asked us to do a Musical Art Program for their morning service. We had taken all the equipment into the main sanctuary and had the majority of it set up when the pastor of the church came up to me and said, "Brother Bridges, they tell me that you are an artist, a poet, and a song writer." I said to him, "Well, I have been called a poet and an artist, but a song writer? That is a new one!"

We both had a good laugh over it and a few days later I thought to myself, if they are going to call me a songwriter, then I had better get busy and write one or two. So, I did write a couple songs and put them in this section of my book... then I went back to painting and writing poems.

It is not hard to tell I don't know that much about writing music, but at least I did try. I did write a few, and the words do have good meanings. The song, *The Babe of Bethlehem*, was sung in our church during the Christmas season. Even if I do say so, I think it turned out pretty good.

The Babe Of Bethlehem

You are the Babe of Bethlehem,
Born on Christmas night.

The angels sang, the Shepherds gazed,
The stars shown oh so bright.
You are the Babe of Bethlehem,
Born on Christmas night.

Holy, holy, what a wondrous sight,
You are the Babe of Bethlehem,
Born on Christmas night.

Some call you Emmanuel,
Others King of Kings.
The Babe that was born on Christmas night,
Is Lord of everything.

Holy, holy, what a wondrous sight,
You are the Babe of Bethlehem,
Born on Christmas night.

He Just Wiped It All Away

I never had a cross to carry,
I never had a crown of thorns.
I never hung on a cross of Calvary,
I wasn't forsaken or forlorn.

They didn't spit on me or curse me,
They didn't even know that I was there.
I was in the crowd just watching,
Without a worry or a care.

Chorus
I cannot tell how much I owe Him for a debt I cannot pay.
But somehow through His great mercy, He wiped it all away.

I never had a purple robe,
Wrapped around me like a King.
An angry crowd has never mocked me,
I've never suffered anything.

I never stood in Pilate's hall,
To answer charges from an angry throng.
I never heard the cry for death,
From so many who were wrong.
(Chorus)

They didn't give to me the bitter gall,
Or thrust a spear into my side.
I didn't cry, "Father forgive them,"
Like Him before He died.

But yet I reap the blessings, of what happened on that day,
From the Christ who died on Calvary, just to wash my sins away.

Precious Blood

The precious blood of Jesus,
Covers all my sins.
The precious blood of Jesus,
Makes me clean within.

The precious blood of Jesus,
The greatest gift I know.
The precious blood of Jesus,
It washed me white as snow.

Chorus
The precious blood of Jesus,
It will set you free.

The precious blood of Jesus,
Spilled on Calvary.
The precious blood of Jesus,
Given just for me.

The precious blood of Jesus,
A river running free.
The precious blood of Jesus,
Still sets the captive free.
(Chorus)

The Cost Of A Coat

He was given a coat of many colors,
He was his father's favorite son.
Consternation ruled his brothers' hearts,
Anguish among them had begun.

Evil ruled the siblings' emotions,
Anxiety tore at each one's heart.
Intensities rained in heavy torrents,
Judgment ripped each son apart.

To be abandoned in a dried out well,
Would the problem really go away?
Or to be sold, to an Egyptian caravan,
Would the bitterness dissipate that day?

Would it all come back to haunt them,
Would not their actions have a price?
Would they not kneel in judgment,
For such a tremendous sacrifice?

What mattered was the outcome,
All things are in God's hand.
He already knew the ending,
Before the scheme began.

-God is good.

Now Israel loved Joseph more than all his children, because he was the son of his old age and he made him a coat of many colors. -Gen 37:3

Ezekiel's Faith

When the Lord called Ezekiel,
To the valley of dry bones.
He went without a congregation,
By faith he went alone.

Ezekiel didn't stop to analyze,
The situation that he saw.
He just looked up to heaven,
And said, "Lord, thou knowest all."

"Lord, thou knowest," said Ezekiel,
"By thy power it shall be."
Then he spoke the words and prophesied,
And behold what did he see?

Upon the bones God put some flesh,
And over that some skin.
Ezekiel's faith didn't fail him then,
For the lack of breath within.

God said, "Son of man, speak these words,
And command thou to the winds.
And tell them thus saith the Lord,
Come fill the slain within."

Ezekiel did as God commanded,
And breath came into them.
And they lived and stood upon their feet,
An army of great men.

Just A Baby

You were just a baby in a manger.

There is no greater gift today,
Than God's own Son and where He lay.
Just a little baby in a manger.

He grew with pain as any child,
Preparing himself, for a weaver's shroud.
Just a little baby in a manger.

They had never counted up the cost,
They never knew what they had lost.
They had crucified a baby from a manger.

And when the years had come and gone,
They realized then that they were wrong.
You were just a little baby from a manger.

And that is why today we sing,
To you our Savior, Lord, and King.
Because you were just a little baby from a manger.

Yes, you were just a little baby from a manger.

I Didn't Know He Was A King

We ran the streets, played boyish games,
He was a friend of mine.
The caravan left our little town,
And I was left behind.
I didn't know He was a King.

I was there at the wedding in Canaan,
I saw him turn the water into wine.
I was amazed, I was stunned, I thought,
Is this man truly human or divine?
I didn't know He was a King.

I heard the roaring clamoring throng,
Coming down the dusty road.
And saw the broken beaten man,
Bearing along, his heavy load.
I didn't know He was a King.

I was one of those on the hillside,
I am sure you have heard it said.
He actually fed five thousand,
With a little boy's fish and bread.
I didn't know He was a King.

I watched them haul in empty nets,
And then at His command.
They cast again and filled their boats,
Who really was this man?
I didn't know He was a King.

I went with orders to the garden,
I had my sword strapped to my side.
I watched him boldly commit himself,
As the others ran away to hide.
I didn't know He was a King.

I also watched the centurion,
Who went to the garden gate.
I stood in obedience, with my Roman spear,
Knowing full well of his fate.
I didn't know He was a King.

They brought him to the judgment hall,
I scoffed and mocked with all the rest.
He is one of yours, I said to them,
Do with him what you think is best.
I didn't know He was a King.

I was there, the soldier climbed the ladder,
And placed the sign above his head.
I didn't know just who he was,
Until I looked up and I read.

"The King of the Jews"

And then humbly I knelt before Him,
I watched the blood run down His side.
I looked into His battered face,
Then I bowed my head and cried.

Please, please, Lord forgive me.
I didn't know, you were a King.

The Prodigal Son

The farmer truly had been blessed,
It was plain for all to see.
He had his cattle and his land,
And two sons there would be.

He had his servants and his maids,
His riches were galore.
His blessings covered him as a shroud,
Like they never had before.

The youngest son came one day,
And from his father did demand.
"I want my portion of this wealth,
My share of all the land."

Brokenhearted though he be,
The father gave consent.
The young son bid them all goodbye,
And into the world he went.

He squandered everything he had,
On fun and sinful play.
Among the swine his senses came,
"Oh, what a fool I've been this day."

"I'll return unto my father's house,
Rejected and poor for all to see.
I'll fall before him on my face,
Unworthy though I be."

From afar the father saw his son,
And joyful did proclaim.
"My son was lost, but now is found,
Return to him his rightful name."

"Go fetch the fatted calf," he cried,
"A feast we will prepare.
"Oh, sound the joyful news," he said,
Oh, sound it everywhere."

"Run, bring to me the purple robe,
Also, bring the golden ring.
Prepare the music and the harps,
For we will dance and sing."

The youngest son, with bitterness,
Could not hold back his tears.
"What have you done for me," he cried,
"For my faithfulness these many years?"

"I know you have been so faithful, son,
A good lad, without a doubt.
But this, my son, was lost you see,
That is why I sing and shout.

Come, join us at the banquet feast,
Put away your doubts and fears.
But remember son, you cannot share my joy,
If you will not share my tears.

He Called The Twelve

Now, Jesus had summoned two brothers,
Mending their nets by the sea.
One was named James, one was named John,
And their father's name was Zebedee.

The Master so gently did call them,
"Will you both come? Come follow me.
Leave your father, your nets and your boat,
Leave everything there by the sea."

Jesus then called out Levi,
"Levi! Leave the customs as they be.
You are to be one of my chosen,
To help spread the gospel for me."

And then He saw Peter and Andrew,
Casting their nets into the sea.
"I will make you both fishers of men,
Lay down your nets, come, follow me."

Phillip was called, and Bartholomew,
And Simon the Canaanite.
All called to follow the Master,
To do His bidding each day and night.

James, the son of Alphaeus,
And Thaddaeus and Thomas were there.
These were the chosen by the Master,
His cross and His burdens to bear.

And then there was Judas Iscariot,
Predestined to do what must be.
To fulfill the plan of redemption,
To fulfill it for you and for me.

These were the twelve who were chosen,
To fulfill God's ordained special plan.
These were the twelve who were chosen,
These twelve, by the Master's hand.

The Rich Young Ruler

He was a rich young ruler,
With a life so secure.
But troubled with anxiety,
And much to endure.

He approached the Master,
With consternation and strife.
"Tell me Lord, what must I do,
That I might gain eternal life?"

You know my commandments,
Go and give to the poor.
"I have kept them from my youth,
Shall I go and give more?"

Yes, sell all that you have,
Then come follow me.
You will gain so much more,
It is what I decree.

But he went away sorrowful,
Much wealth he had laid aside.
He may well have lost his soul,
To keep his money and his pride.

How hardly shall they that have riches enter into the kingdom of God.
–Mark 10:23

Judge Not

Why do I judge my brother,
With a speck that is in my eye?
When I know not his sorrow,
Nor do I understand his sigh.

I know not of his anguish,
Never see the tears that fall.
With no conception that God above,
Is the ultimate judge of all.

So, if I have nothing else to do,
But be the judge of those who sin.
I think it is best at my own home,
That is where I should begin.

In my house made of glass,
When I am all alone.
Maybe it is best for me,
If I throw not one stone.

-Matt 7:1-5

John Three Sixteen

There was a man named Nicodemus,
The same came to Jesus by night.
To question the Master's teachings,
Of things that didn't seem quite right.

"We know that you are a teacher,
A man that is full of God's love.
For no man can do what you do,
Unless he first comes from God above."

Jesus then said to Nicodemus,
Verily, verily, I say unto thee.
Except a man be born again,
God's kingdom he will never see.

This puzzled the wise old ruler,
And he said, "Lord, how can this be?
How can I enter into my mother's womb?
I am old and gray as you can see."

Jesus answered and said unto him,
Art thou a great ruler of Israel?
And ye know not about these things,
Is that where your wisdom doth fail?

Nicodemus, this I say unto you,
We speak that we know and have seen.
And yet if ye have not the witness,
How can I tell you of Heavenly things?

You see, no man has ascended to Heaven,
Except that he first come from God above.
And I Nicodemus, the Son of man,
I came to you with His love.

For God so loved this very world,
That I, His only Son, He did send.
And whosoever believeth in me,
Will dwell forever in the Master's hand.

For I wasn't sent to condemn you,
But through me you can be free.
And you, Nicodemus, of all rulers,
Do you not believe in me?

He that believeth is not condemned,
But he that believeth not, so will be.
The condemnation that rests on that man,
Will last for all eternity.

These were the sayings of Jesus,
To Nicodemus a Pharisee.
Not only were they spoken for the ruler,
But also, for you and me.

Remember Me

Take this bread and think of me,
The Son of God, hanging on a tree.

And knowing that I carried there,
All your sins and griefs to bear.

Your heartache and your pain was mine,
I carried in a moment of time.

So, take my child, and eat this bread,
And remember my words and what I said.

Then take this cup, my blood was shed,
From the crown of thorns upon my head.

From the Roman sword that pierced my side,
Blood fell for you, that was why I died.

So, remember me, when the table's spread,
And you drink this cup and eat this bread.

I did this because I love you.

The Cross

The Cross I cannot comprehend,
The price on Calvary paid.
Sins and burdens, that I carried,
At the foot of it was laid.

The blood that ran, like torrents,
At the foot of the Cross, it congealed.
The Son had paid my ransom,
My destiny, it was sealed.

What love, the Father has given,
What a sacrifice He gave that day.
Like a cleansing celestial fountain,
He has washed my sins away.

What a great God we serve.

Who Is This Christ

Who is this Christ,
Called God's own Son,
Who walked the shores of time?

Who is this Christ,
Abused and crucified,
So pure and so divine?

Who is this Christ,
The incarnate,
The mystery of mankind?

Who is this Christ,
Laid in a borrowed tomb,
Then left His shroud behind?

Who is this Christ,
As He knelt and prayed,
Said not my will, but thine?

Who is this Christ?
I will tell you who,
I am His and He is mine.

Was It Worth Your Time

How many times have I wondered Lord,
When you walked the shores of Galilee.
Was it really worth your time,
The time you spent for me?

Or when you stood in Pilate's hall,
The humiliation for all to see.
The time you stood before him, Lord,
Was that time spent just for me?

And when they nailed you to the cross,
While you hung on Calvary.
Was it really worth your time,
The time you spent for me?

And the times you spent in prayer,
Those long hours in Gethsemane.
Was it really worth your time,
The time you spent for me?

And then I have to ask myself,
What have I done for thee?
I ask you, Lord, was it worth your time,
The time you spent for me?

The Blood

I know it's not a pleasant thing,
To talk about the blood of Christ.
That fell on Herod's marble floors,
At such a horrific sacrifice.

It makes one cringe to talk of the crown,
That pierced the skull of God's dear son.
That caused the blood to run in torrents,
To lie in pools, upon the ground to run.

I cannot escape the blood that fell,
That flowed in matted hair.
I also must share the blood of Christ,
And the Cross I, too, must bear.

If I am to be His witness,
Of the blood that was shed that day.
Then I must recognize the price,
And be willing that price to pay.

For this is the blood... -Matt 26:28

The Robe

They took my robe and cast their lots,
And replaced it with a cross.
It was what I wore that day,
For a world condemned and lost.

The wandering road that led to Calvary,
Was not like the road today.
It was strewn with righteous rebels,
As Roman soldiers led the way.

The cross became so heavy,
It was more than I could bear.
The only shroud I had for a covering,
Was your sins I had to wear.

Though some mocked me and they chanted,
And some wept along the way.
The price for your redemption,
Was all I wore that day.

Marked For Me

He walked the shores of Galilee,
And left footprints in the sand.
He hung on a cross on Golgotha,
And left nail prints in His hands.

He said, "With you I will always be,
With you, I will abide."
To prove His true commitment,
He left a sword mark in His side.

The scars upon His sweaty brow,
They didn't really have to be.
Yet they marked Him with a crown,
And that was for you and me.

Consider the marks of the Master,
Wait patiently for His call.
The marks were left for you and me,
That makes Him Lord of all.

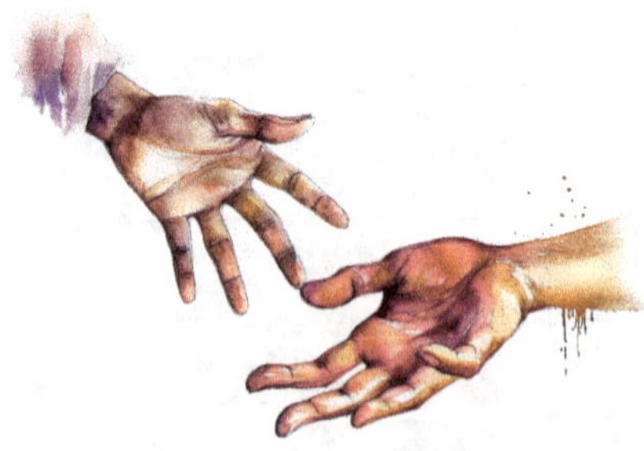

The Lowly Man From Galilee

They said they were searching for a king,
They wanted a king to set them free.
Could he have really been the one? The lowly man from Galilee?

They said he turned the water into wine,
And he made a blind man see.
Was he the one of whom Isaiah spoke,
The lowly man from Galilee?

And he fed five thousand at one time,
And cast out demons, they did agree.
You think he could really be the one,
The lowly man from Galilee?

I heard he even raised the dead,
And walked upon the sea.
I do believe he is who he said he is,
The lowly man from Galilee.

It is recorded, they shouted and sang,
"Hosanna, King of Kings you will be."
And then they spit upon his face,
The lowly man from Galilee.

They mocked Him and nailed Him to a cross,
On a hill call Mount Calvary.
And yet they hailed him as a king,
The lowly man from Galilee.

Will they yet have another chance, for one so great as He?
Yes! Before He left earth, He said, *I will return*,
And He will... The King of Galilee.

He Could Have

He could have stopped the soldiers,
At Gethsemane's entrance gate.
But yet He knelt in prayer,
Knowing full well of His fate.

He could have called ten thousand angels,
To show His royal authority.
But in agony, He just hung there,
And took the pain for you and me.

He could have laid the cross aside,
And said, it is not for me to bear.
But the weight He bore was for us,
And yet we do not care.

There are many things He could have done,
Upon that destined day.
But He only had you and me in mind,
As they came in force and led Him away.

We trample the blood of God's own Son,
Without a worry or a care.
While His word lies covered in a coat of dust,
And we have no time for prayer.

Yes, there are so many things,
He could have done....

Who Built The Cross

History has recorded many things,
That we will never understand.
I wonder, who built the Cross,
Who really was that man?

Yes, many times, I've wondered,
Who built the Cross for Christ?
Where God's own Son would hang one day,
At such a horrific sacrifice.

Who cut the tree, who carved the wood,
Who designed the Cross for blood?
Who dug the hole for the masterpiece,
And sunk it in the mud?

Who built the Cross? Who built the Cross?
Did he even begin to understand?
Upon that Cross, upon a lonely hill,
Would hang a guiltless man.

Who built the Cross? Who built the Cross?
I doubt that we will ever know.
But without it, my sins would never be,
Washed as white as snow.

~ Eight ~

POEMS OF INSPIRATION

Section Contents

The poems that are set in this section are from my collection of miscellaneous poems I had written over the years. They really are not in any particular order. Some are prayers. Some are simply thoughts I had about God or questions I was pondering at the time. Sometimes I wrote poems challenging myself to grow in my relationship with God.

Maybe you will have some of the same questions, and maybe some will challenge you, too. I hope they bring inspiration and...
I hope you enjoy them.

My Prayer

Holy Spirit, I want to thank you,
For your presence throughout this day.
And I want to tell you that I love you,
As I prepare my heart to pray.

I'll need to take a moment, Lord,
To search deep within my heart.
Just to be sure, throughout this day,
I have truly fulfilled my part.

To be assured, there is no condemnation,
As I kneel before your throne.
So I can cherish these few moments,
That we can share alone.

As I enter into your sacred realms,
My petitions to you I bring.
And these you know, before I ask,
For you, Lord, know everything.

But as your child, you want me here,
To be humble at your feet.
To never forget Lord, who you are,
And the place where we should meet.

You are El Shaddai, Almighty God,
The bright and morning star.
Ruler of my heart - Adonai,
Lord, you truly are who you are.

Time

How many times have I said, Lord,
I need to take some time to pray.
But yet I am so busy,
I will another day.

The things in life are pressing,
The world has slowly slithered in.
I'm really doing my best, Lord,
To keep my heart from sin.

I know that you protect,
And keep me day by day.
So tomorrow I am going to try,
To take some time to pray.

But I wonder...

What if tomorrow doesn't come,
And, before you, what would I say?
I think it is best if I take the time, Lord,
To bow my head and pray.

His Grace

His grace that pardons,
And covers my sins.
His grace that has redeemed,
And filled me within.

It flows like a river,
Like a stream will always be.
Sufficient forever,
I know, sufficient for me.

How deep does His grace,
How deep does it flow?
Could a mortal like me,
Understand or even know?

Comprehension does not register,
The depths of His grace.
Only then will I understand it,
When we stand... face to face.

My House Of Glass

It is a grand house that I now possess,
Quite unique, it is made of glass.
Adequate room for things of the future,
But now filled with things of the past.

One can see through my house of glass,
So what I say and do, it really doesn't matter.
Should I propel pebbles of slander, gossip of stone?
I am sure my house of glass would then shatter.

Could I then rebuild my house of glass,
From all the damage that I had done?
No, for everyone is given a house of glass,
And if destroyed, you only get one.

Character

I will be, years from now,
What I am today.
The only difference that will be,
Is what I read and what I say.

What I watch, the friends I make,
Will characterize who I am.
Years from now, not today,
Will typify what kind of man.

I must gingerly guard my character,
As a priceless gem, stored away.
Then I can be, years from now,
What I am today.

I Would If I Could

You tell me that you love me,
And you seek my will each day.
But yet, you cannot remember,
When was the last time you did pray.

You quote my word to those in need,
And seldom get it right.
Because you fail to search my word,
Each morning and each night.

And if I were to ask you,
From my word, what did you glean today?
Would you hang your head in shame,
With nothing from your lips to say?

Does it not disturb you, my child,
The calm you once had is gone.
The joy from your soul has waned,
And from your heart there is no song.

And when that friend in trouble asked,
Will you remember me when you pray?
You could not really intercede,
Because we had not met that day.

That is why, I cannot bear your burdens,
And I cannot calm your fears.
I cannot weep for you, my child,
Because up here, there are no tears.

Just Three Little Words

Just three little words,
They are so hard to say.
Just three little words,
But needs said every day.
I love you.

Just three little words,
Spoken from your heart.
Just three little words,
But you must do your part.
I love you.

Just three little words,
Tell them, before it's too late.
Just three little words,
Needs to be said to your mate.
I love you.

Just three little words,
To say them... So hard to do.
Just three little words,
I would say them, if I were you.
I love you.

Just three little words,
Whisper them, when you pray.
It's just three little words,
But it will change your day.

Just say it - *I love you.*

I Wonder

If I had been called to follow Him,
Would I have laid my nets aside?
Or if I was in the chanting crowd,
Would I also have cried, Crucify!
I wonder.

If I were in the garden,
As He alone knelt down to pray.
Would I have been impervious,
As they led my Christ away?
I wonder.

If I had stood afar and gazed,
At the scene on Golgotha Hill.
I have often thought to myself,
Just what anguish would I feel?
I wonder.

If I had been the one approached,
With the bag of silver change.
Would history record the same of me,
A traitor, greedy, and deranged?

There are a lot of things
... that I wonder.
.... I wonder.

Which Way To The Cross

I was weary, alone, in despair I asked,
"Sir, can you tell me the way to the Cross?"
He also looked weary, forlorn, and sad,
"No," he said, "My friend, I too am lost."

Traveling a bit further and still quite confused,
I approached an old woman with her heavy load.
"Can you tell me the way to the Cross?" I asked.
She said, "Just somewhere down this long, dusty road."

Ah! A fine gentleman, I said to myself,
How thankful I am that he came along.
"Sir, can you tell me how I can get to the Cross?"
"I could try my friend, but plausibly I would be wrong."

I was determined to get to the Cross,
There was nothing left, but misery and pain.
It seemed as if no one knew the way,
Was what the Master went through, truly in vain??

And then one day I read of the nail scarred hands,
And the marks from the crown on His head.
I read of the place where the Master laid,
And the place where they presumed Him dead.

And then I realized that I knew all the time,
I knew the way to the Cross.
It had already been paved with the blood of God's Son,
A clear reminder that no one would be lost.

If

If I am to be your comforter,
And abide with you each day.
Then I will know the things you do,
And listen to the things you say.

I'll have to watch the things you watch,
Rather they're good or things unkind.
I will know every inappropriate thought,
That dwells within your mind.

Remember, I will not let you offend me,
By what you say and what you do.
I created you a free moral agent,
The choice is up to you.

I'll Be There

If you fast and pray and seek me,
I'll be there.
In humbleness and broken spirit,
I'll be there.
For your loved ones and your problems,
I will listen to your prayer.
If you fast and pray and seek me,
I'll be there.

In the secret room together,
We'll be there.
All your burdens and your sorrows,
We will share.
With a heart that is pure and tender,
My child, be prepared.
For if you fast and pray and seek me,
I'll be there.

He Didn't Have To

He didn't have to take the pain,
He could have walked away.
But it was you, He had in mind,
When He went to the Cross that day.

Will you flaunt His horrible sacrifice,
And just go your jovial way?
Not conscious of the price He paid,
Neither listening to what He has to say.

I wonder ...?

-Written for a friend who said, "I don't have time for that religious stuff."

Who

Who is this Holy Spirit,
The essence of God's own Son.
Who is this Holy Spirit,
The balance of the three in one.

Who is this one who walks beside me,
And guides me day by day.
And helps me weigh my every thought,
And guards me with what I have to say.

This precious gift from heaven,
I cannot comprehend.
That guides me with every step I take,
And keeps my heart from sin.

I may not understand it,
But this one thing I know.
My sins are covered by His blood,
And washed as white as snow.

Doubt Not

If the wind cannot be seen,
But yet every day it blows.
It becomes a fact, there is a wind,
This, everybody knows.

The sun shines oh so brightly,
And no doubt we feel the heat.
But the heat, did you ever see it?
Can you describe to me how neat?

And how amusing and utterly amazing,
You and I have never seen the sound.
But every day we hear it,
So it must be, it has to be, somewhere around.

Oh yes, I heard you say, you had friendship,
Wow, is that something I can hold?
Can I touch it or can I see it?
But yet, it's more precious than pure gold.

And there are days I stand and gaze,
Into the sky that is so blue.
And I ask, what is sky? It has no substance,
But yet there is sky, it is true.

And what about this God in heaven,
I will ask, how can that be?
I have never seen His majestic abode,
Although His word reveals it to me.

You see, there are numerous things that we believe,
Not by sight, but by feel and sound.
We cannot see them, nor can we touch them,
But we know that they are around.

So this realm, I cannot see nor touch,
I will not doubt there is a God above.
Who watches over me every day,
And covers me with his illustrious love.

There will always be things I cannot comprehend,
And that is what makes life worth living.
So until my Lord says, come home my child,
I am going to keep loving and giving.

How Many Times

How many times can we grieve you Lord,
And yet you linger near.
How many times must we have our way,
And walk in doubt and fear.

How many times can we turn from you,
And say, "You will still be there."
How many times can we cry and pout,
And whimper, "God, you are not fair."

How many times can we fool ourselves,
As if it is a game we play.
How many times will you hear us say,
"I'll try again another day."

Well, I do think you have a limit Lord,
Whatever that may be.
It is best we lay all at your Cross,
For now Lord, and all eternity.

Bones Under A Stone

There is nothing quite so lamentable,
As a pile of bones under a stone.
Long, long ago forgotten,
Lying there silently and all alone.

Years have come and many gone,
And now, no one really cares.
There is no more crying, no more moaning,
Ringing of the hands, nor wiping of the tears.

All the deeds, in a span of life accomplished,
Whether remembered as bad or good.
We will all be bones under a stone,
Just lying there, in a box of wood.

What profits a man, if he gains the whole world and then loses his soul?? -Matt 16:26

I will admit, I shed a tear as I wrote this.

The Children Of The Mines

So much is recorded in history,
Most forgotten and left behind.
Have you ever heard or wondered,
Who were the *Children of the Mines?*

So when we read of days gone by,
These are the nuggets that we find.
Stories read and then abandoned,
Like the *Children of the Mines.*

It was so many, many years ago,
And how soon we all forget.
About the little ragged children,
So cold, so damp, and wet.

Taken from their beds at dawn,
Some only four or five.
Under nourished, so frail and pale,
Some barely kept alive.

It wasn't, just ten or twenty, no,
It was thousands that we read.
To bring the coal out of the mines,
To meet the greedy masters' needs.

They were hooked in little harnesses,
Like wretched little mules.
To haul the coal out of the mines,
To satisfy the greedy fools.

Some seven years old, from Derbyshire,
Some five and six, from Bradford and Lees.
Some recorded as young as four years old,
Coming from the collieries.

Not all were boys, some were girls,
Treated with disgust and shame.
So the greedy, monstrous owners,
Could have their wealth and fame.

They drove the carts with girdles,
Yes, even with the chains.
Hauling coal out of the mines,
For their masters, who had no shame.

I could go on, there's no place to stop,
The stories are sad, and they are true.
Recorded in the books of time,
I am writing them again for you.

It's just another part of history,
We read with sadness and regret.
Annals, with withered torn pages,
To remind us, lest we forget.

So I will end this story now,
And I do wish it wasn't true.
But these are the facts, recorded,
And I send them on to you.

Without a doubt, a sad part of our culture,
And I know it's been a long, long time.
But my heart still aches, just the same,
To read of the *Children of the Mines*.

The Mighty Always Fall

Let us start at the beginning,
The way it was meant to be.
For men to love each other,
And live in perfect harmony.

But power became an evil force,
That stretched across the land.
And tyrant leaders set the stage,
To control their fellow man.

Mighty nations did arise,
To power by the sword.
One thing they seemed to all forget,
Who was Master, who was Lord.

The kings of ages, though dark they be,
Had all in their control.
We own the world, they did proclaim,
We own man's very soul.

Consider the mighty Egyptians who said,
There is no better way.
Pharoah is God, we'll live like this,
Each and every day.

We read of the Meads and the Persians,
They knew what they could do.
We'll have the Babylonian Kingdom,
It will be ours in a night or two.

What happened to Alexander?
He is the great, they said.
Immortal though he contrived to be,
Alexander – He is dead!

Oh yes, Mussolini, where are you?
How you did tirade and rage.
You controlled your loyal subjects,
Like animals in a cage.

The Israelites, they had their say,
No one dare take our land.
After all, our King is the living God,
We fear not the power of man.

The powerful Roman Empire,
Set the stage in full array.
You will bow before this kingdom,
All will bow, this very day.

Hitler in his pomp and pride,
Spread his hands out before the world.
It is power I have, power I possess,
My plans are now unfurled.

Let us take a look at our own land,
And ask God, what can we do?
To take back our morals and dignity,
Before we relinquish everything, too.

Because if you, my friend, are so naïve,
To think that this can never be.
Then you had better dust off your books,
And go reread your History.

What Is Evil

What is evil?
The greed of the heart,
The lust of the mind.
Concern for oneself,
None at all for mankind.

What is evil?
An act of depravity,
Vileness, sin, and demand.
It had a beginning,
But yet, has no end.

What is evil?
A lack of compassion,
Void of embrace.
Emotions that are lethargic,
Smirking at disgrace.

What is evil?
The master of deception,
The power of control.
The bid for man's body,
The prize is his soul.

Will We Ever Learn

Will we learn anything from history,
Will we learn anything from the past?
How kingdoms gained such wealth and power,
How so many didn't even last.

In antiquity we read of Joseph,
His Jehovah helped make Egypt great.
From the writing of Herodotus,
We can study of their fate.

Chaldeans account of the deluge,
The descent of Ishtar to Hades.
After Gyges and Ashurbanipal,
Brought purity to its knees.

We learn nothing from Phoenician,
Or from the short reign of Hiram.
Villages with the fortified walls,
Became the sacrificial lamb.

Time will not permit me,
To reminisce of every nation's fate.
America, we had better wake up fast,
And maybe now, it is too late.

There are so many, many warnings,
History has recorded for us all.
Don't think one moment, we are immune,
Arrogance and pride is always before the fall.

Evaluation

We laugh, we mock, we have our fun,
In lethargy, we go our gregarious way.
Convictions have taken wings of flight,
We are deaf to what God has to say.

His word lies on tables, covered with dust,
Pages warn only with yellow stains.
Our eyes glazed over, by worldly appeal,
We are imprudent infants, half insane.

Our minds have slowly been invaded,
With improper wants and carnal greed.
We have morphed into wretched zombies,
Oblivious we are, to others needs.

What God will do to America,
No doubt, is subject of intense debate.
Wake up! Wake up! You foolish nation,
Wake up! Before it is too late.

What Is Love

We all describe it, and we affirm it,
We apply it to our daily lives.
It is used in so many ways,
Sometimes with deceit and with lies.

You say you love, and then you hurt,
You lie, you cheat and steal.
Actions are so very clear and loud,
Can't you see the pain and how others feel?

Because love is gentle, it is kind,
It gives when others covet greed.
It is filled with honest emotions,
It doesn't take, it gives to others' needs.

Love heals the body and the heart,
It heals the soul; it heals the mind.
Controls all wants and all emotions,
Spews forth compassion, is always kind.

Love sheds a tear, when others hurt,
Wraps arms with tender care.
It gives, it grieves, it discerns, it feels,
It is sacred, it is something we can share.

So what is love, you ask me,
It comes from God above.
It is truly the essence of the three in one,
So love is... just plain love.

Your Love

Lord, people say you did not die,
Just for me alone.
And there isn't even such a thing,
As a God upon a throne.

Some say the world has always been,
Perhaps a million years or so.
And there never was a place called hell,
Where all the wicked go.

And Heaven, well they scoff at that,
And mock your saints who pray.
They eat and drink and have their fun,
And say, we'll all just die some day.

But in my heart, there is a peace,
That could only come from God above.
I thank you for your gift of grace,
And your never failing love.

Precious Memories

At the vale of the snowcap mountain,
Resting beside the running stream.
I closed my eyes in meditation,
And soon drifted into dream.

White cumulus clouds had parted,
My Lord was standing there.
His eyes were blue and misty,
Sunbeams floating in His hair.

A moment there He lingered,
So lovely and so still.
I gazed on Him, mercy flowed,
My eyes began to fill.

Nail prints, prominent in His hands,
And marks of scars around His head.
Where they placed on Him the crown of thorns,
I envisioned the place where they claimed Him dead.

And then He ascended to Heaven's loft,
On clouds as white as snow.
Don't cry my child, I will return,
I just wanted you to know.

Quiescent - /qwhy-ESS-ent/. To be quiet, resting, still. Like the quiescent moments lying in a hammock on a beautiful warm day.

I **Seek His Will**

Confined in the realm of His presence,
I seek and search what is to be.
Oft times, I find when I am quiescent,
That is when He reveals most to me.

Not always what is revealed is most pleasant,
There are some things I would rather not see.
But yet, if I want His full blessing,
Then that is the way it must be.

I must yield to Him my intentions,
I must consent to Him complete control.
I must give to Him my full devotion,
That involves my body and soul.

Then when I have met His requirements,
And I walk in the light He has given to me.
I will then receive God's full blessing,
That He has in store for me.

Sunrise

Some times in the evening,
When the sun begins to fall.
There will come a time of sorrow,
It will come for one and all.

But in the morning, there's the sunrise,
It will take away some of the despair.
For we will know our loved one's smiling,
In a better place, somewhere over there.

So take comfort in the sunrise,
Think of the bright things left behind.
Dwell on your loved one's happy times,
And may some joy in that you find.

Are You There

To be honest with you, Lord,
There are times when I wonder if you're there.
And because I'm only human, Lord,
There are times I wonder even if you care.

There are times that I do question,
Some of the things that happen in my life.
Why are there days of pain and sorrow,
Why are there days of tears and strife?

I have thought to myself so many times,
If I could only hear you say.
Well done, my child, how proud I am,
Of what you have said and done today.

What have I done? What have I said?
Well, Lord, I do need to reminisce.
It may be I, who am at fault,
There may be something that I miss.

In my time and devotions, rendered to you,
Half-hearted at times they seem to be.
I think I know the answer, Lord,
I think the answer lies in me.

Purify

Skim away the dross, Lord,
All impurities refine.
So when I kneel in prayer,
It is not my will, but thine.

Shroud me in your glory,
Keep my heart pure for you.
Protect me from the wiles of sin,
In everything I do.

Purify my heart, Lord,
Begin a work in me.
A vessel fit for service,
That I will always be.

Refined

From the depths of my impurity,
At last I have been refined.
He has claimed me as His child,
Forever His and He is mine.

From the furnace of affliction,
I am free, yes free at last.
Redeemed by Calvary's gift to me,
All is eradicated from the past.

My heart shall sing His praises,
I will relish in His grace.
Hold Him in adoration,
Until I see Him face to face.

What love it is, He has given,
For such a wretch as me.
Should I not daily praise Him,
And a witness always be?

...I think so.

Isaiah 48:10

Who Am I

Who am I, that you would abandon,
Your celestial throne on high.
Take on the form of humanity,
For such an abhorrent one, as I.

To bear the whip that ripped the flesh,
And tore the skin to shreds.
You who had all authority,
But still took the pain instead.

Who am I who has no time,
To kneel before your throne.
To relish in your love and grace,
And spend time with you alone.

Look down to me, your child, Lord,
From the heights of your habitation.
Let me never, never, forget the price,
That was paid for my salvation.

I Know

In my secret closet,
I know God is always there.
To intercede in my hour with Him,
To listen to my prayer.

When He inclines my heart to pray,
He has an ear to hear.
To Him there is music in a groan,
There is beauty in a fallen tear.

There is solace in His presence,
Tranquility covers like a shroud.
My heart is filled with adoration,
Knowing I am His child.

~ Nine ~

WRAPPING UP IN FUN

Section Contents

Well, this just about wraps up my *life in thought and poem*. Now, there is one area that I have always tried to keep in my life so I thought it should be included in this book, and that is - keeping a good sense of humor. Of course, you have probably already caught onto that in some of the other stories.

Sometimes, I would write poems when a funny thing happened, or I had a random thought or curiosity. Sometimes I would write poems for friends -- or just to keep myself from getting bored in my old age. You young people just wait...your day is coming and then you'll understand what I was talking about.

Nuts

I just knew some day I'd write a poem,
That would make no sense at all.
My mind would be a total blank,
With nothing in my skull.

I'd sit and scratch my head a bit,
And wonder what to write.
What did I do today, will do tomorrow,
What did I do last night?

Did I tell my good wife I love her,
Did I thank her for my meal?
Did I just sit the day away,
Did I forget to take my pill?

I guess it really doesn't matter,
I am having myself a ball.
It is me I gotta live with,
And I don't mind myself at all.

Thank You Mr. Edison

Sometimes when I am just looking around,
There are certain things that appeal to me.
Take that light pole, over there,
I think, *How can that be?*

We just take things for granted,
That they will always be.
A light at night to shine our way,
On land or on the sea.

I do complain when the light bill's come,
And say, "This one I will not pay."
But I always do, I have no choice,
I usually pay that very day.

I guess I am so very grateful,
What more can I really say?
Just, thank you Mr. Edison,
For what you did that day.

And if I should meet you on the street,
I will gladly shake your hand.
Flipping a switch upon my wall,
Sure beats burning candles at both ends.

This I attached to my workshop door:

Please Return My Tools!

If I am borrowed by a friend,
Right welcome shall he be.
To use to get his work done with,
But to be returned, you see.

It's not imparted knowledge,
Nor treasures that I store.
But tools I find when often lent,
Return back here no more.

Ol' Jake

Boys! Let's get Ol' Jake, that old hound dog,
Go spread the word around.
They say Ol' Jake's been seen again,
He be somewhere back in d'town.

He now gonna pay for all he's done,
Ya bet, his reckonin' day is here.
Me, m'self not seen 'im yet,
But de' say, he be somewhere neer.

Ol' Susie Jones say he ain't been d'ere.
Trashy Sally say d'same.
And Mary Beth, you kant trust her,
Both d'em girls is half insane.

So we's gonna tear d'is town apart,
Ol' Jake, d'ere is no place you kin hide.
We be lookin' for you, boy,
We gonna be lookin' all far and wide.

Cause now d'whole town be knowin',
D'at horrible thang you did.
You not be foolin' us anymore, Ol' Jake,
We all know.... *It is yo' kid!*

Just Thinking

You know what, I'm a happy boy,
Sitting here, thinking of years gone by.
Thinking of things I want to do,
Before I up and die.

I want to take a trip back home,
And see where I used to play.
And maybe see my hairless cat,
That ran away one day.

I'd throw rocks in the old fishpond,
If by now not full of trash.
And sit and scratch myself again,
From the old huckleberry rash.

And where is old yeller, that dog,
Who couldn't tree a coon.
All she was really good for,
Was just howling at the moon.

Susie Brown, what happened to her?
Man, she was an ugly thing.
But wow, she had a set of lungs,
And could that gal ever sing.

Well, I could just keep going,
My brain is full of stuff.
But I'm gonna stop now for a break,
I think I've said enough!

This poem is on the silly side, but I awoke one night and this crazy poem was running through my head from a dream I had. Besides that, you really don't have to read it if you choose not to... but you probably will because it is so bad and you are curious. *It's just a dream...*

Just A Dream

Such a void, just an illusion, was it real or just a dream,
Was there any real conclusion? There was none that it seemed.

Thoughts scattered in flight, sensations floating in the air,
In the dark of the night, was I here or was I there?

But I must have that card, the card I must possess,
It has to come back, to be with the rest.

What kind of a card with such mystical powers,
That allotted my time into no days or no hours.

Flung into animation, no rhythm nor rhyme,
Nothing but satirical, sending chills up my spine.

I ran through the streets, searching each hideous face,
Looking for my card, with disgust and disgrace.

Give it back, you evil villain, I demand of my card,
It is valuable and it's rare, and I have searched long and hard.

Ah, said he, I have placed it in my room with great care,
Up the narrow winding stairs, true, I have hidden it there.

The room was a vapor, it was neither here nor was it there,
Doors suspended in space, appeared floating in air.

Nostalgic beings, all searching hard and long for my card,
Along secret passageways, they sought long and hard.

Then in a foggy vapor, there appeared an old man,
He had a strange gold medallion, held tight in his hand.

It's the price for the card, said he, with a mean vicious grin,
Wake up, it's just an illusion, with no beginning or end.

No! I said, it's my card, it's the one that I had,
It's a rare old card, given to me from my dad.

So give it back to me, you place it back in my hand,
So this stupid, dumb dream can soon come to an end.

It was an old Tarot Card, he held in his old, withered hand,
But not just any old card, the thing was worth fifty grand.

Could I have been so possessed, with something that small,
Because at the end of my dream, it was really nothing at all.

To My Friend Troy, Who Is Moving On

There once was a frog,
From the land of Salone.
Who made a great leap,
Into the world of unknown.

He left other frogs behind,
And left them quite sad.
But in the end, his decision,
Wasn't really that bad.

But God had a reason,
Because He's so good and so kind.
And in the end, it was better,
Than what he left behind.

So my friend, don't you worry,
What the future will be.
Everything's in His hands,
On that we both will agree.

Written to our friend, Joyce Boren, after the publication of her book of poems in December 2011.

From Me To You

From one poet to another,
I think your book is fine.
But I have to be real honest,
It is not as good as mine.

I like the story of your life,
The revealing of your heart.
The truth that most would never share,
The things that tore your life apart.

And then you wrote of healing,
And the power of His love.
You told of His redeeming grace,
And hope that comes from God above.

That's what makes your book so special,
Written to touch some broken heart.
Telling others of God's faithfulness,
Contrite in spirit, willing to do our part.

My daughter asked me what in the world made me write this poem -and was the church trying to collect money for socks?? I laughed and told her, *no*, one Sunday at church, Wally was on the platform wearing mismatched socks. I was razzing him about it, then went home and wrote this to give him a good laugh.

Socks

What can one say about an old pair of socks,
Full of holes that should be thrown away.
To give to the needy? I don't think so,
So, in your old dresser drawer they just stay.

You wear them to work and even to church,
And then in the pulpit you act so forlorn.
Just because you have on those nasty old socks,
Full of holes, worn out and all torn.

I would be ashamed to get up and complain,
With all the money we have to pay.
And I sure ain't buying you more than one pair,
I don't care if you wear the stinking things every day.

I am trying to be real nice with the dilemma you're in,
Like some of the others, I feel kinda bad.
So, I'll spend a few bucks and buy you a new pair,
But I want you to know, Wally, I think I've been had.

Little Green Worms

What can I say about fuzzy green worms,
That I just happened to stick on this page.
There's nothing to say, my mind's gone a blank,
Green Worms I hear, just ain't the rage.

There just is no way you can train them,
I know for a fact they are not fit to eat.
For sure you don't want fuzzy green worms,
Crawling around at your ankles and feet.

You can't put them on chains to hang on your neck,
They're not good for dangling on your ears.
You can't give them for gifts, to just any old friend,
And you dare not even think of your peers.

So all I can say is, I'll make this poem short,
And I'll not bore you with dumb silly lines.
If walking along and you see those green things,
Take one look and leave them behind!

Just Thinking Time Away

I'll think of things that makes no sense,
Of things when I was just a lad.
I'll think of things I never did,
Of things I never had.

To me that's so important,
Rather than wasting time away.
Gives my good wife the break she needs,
Trying to understand the the things I say.

So, until my brain rejuvenates,
And I can jot a line or two.
I will just end it for today,
And send it on to you.

You may not understand me,
But my old friends -*they will.*
They have the same old frame of mind,
From popping all those pills.

We are just a happy bunch,
Doing what old folks do.
Because our mind's a total blank,
There is never nothing new.

-That's why I'm not typing anymore,
I'll say this day is through!

Have a good day –

And a couple as food for thought...

The Color Of Your Eyes

When we had our first encounter,
And I looked into your eyes.
I did not see the color,
Much to my surprise.

I did not see if they were brown,
Green or gray or blue.
For when I looked into your eyes,
All I saw was you.

There was a twinkle in your eyes,
But the color I did not see.
All I noticed were your eyes,
Intensely looking back at me.

So when I look at God's creation,
And all I see is the color of skin.
And do not see my brother's eyes,
Nor see the hurt and pain within.

Then it is I, who has the problem,
And I must search my heart within.
For God only sees us as his children,
And He sees us all, made just like Him.

Spring

Death has taken its winter toll,
Wherever one looks, it is all around.
Brackish water, stagnant ponds,
Withered grass upon the ground.

Trees and azaleas look so forlorn,
Roses and spiraeas with droopy leaves.
Brown moss covers garden rocks,
No life among the trees.

Frozen ponds with captive fish,
Lifeless beneath the frozen ice.
Squirrels happily nestled in hollow trees,
Covered bark in winter lice.

Then spring breaks forth with nature's shout,
Budding trees, luscious plants in full array.
Rodents emerge from burrowed holes,
To see the dawning of the day.

So there is life everywhere,
Life springs forth and joy abounds.
Robins chatter, birds sing in flight,
It is heaven's and nature's sounds.

So after death, then there is life,
And such beauty to behold.
A saying quoted a million times,
Life is more precious than pure gold.

I Knew It

I really think I'm getting old,
Maybe a bit insane.
I keep trying to write myself some poems,
But nothing's in my brain.

I just sit and think and scratch my head,
Trying to make things rhyme.
Knowing all the while doing it,
It is a waste of time.

I knew someday, I'd write a poem,
That would make no sense at all.
My mind would be a total blank,
With nothing in my skull.

Thoughts keep running through my head,
And I'll type a word or two.
Then I lose my train of thought,
And don't know what to do.

I'll think of things when I was young,
And try to express and to relate.
And in the middle of doing it,
I'll forget the time and date.

I'll start to tell of things I had,
And what happened when just a kid.
And then I'll just stare into space,
I'll forget everything I did.

I really can't explain it,
I don't know if I even care.
My eyes are dim, my hearing's gone,
But thank the Lord, I still have hair.

It bothers me not, if this makes no sense,
And you think, *That boy's lost his mind.*
I, myself, am having fun, and it's better,
Than just sitting on my behind.

So as long as I am able,
To type a word or two.
You all may think I am senile,
But it is just what I'm going to do.

You may read them if you want to,
Me? I'm just passing time away.
I am sure before they put me under,
I'll write again, another day.

Poor Bev

Bev was at her wits today,
Her compassion was showing through.
But she really almost lost it,
And said, "I just don't know what to do with you."

My twin brother came to see me,
We were laughing and having a ball.
Then she took away my mirror,
And said, "You fool, that isn't him at all."

Well, how did I know it wasn't him,
Don't twins most times look the same?
He had the same old wrinkles,
And he looked a bit insane.

Oh well, it's just one of those days,
Tomorrow will be another.
When she's not home, I'll look again,
To make sure it's not my brother.

Fun Day

Got a little bored today,
Didn't know what to do.
Take a stroll through the woods,
Or read a book or two?

So I went out and built a snowman,
Brought him in, set him by the door.
Barely turned my back on him,
He started peeing on the floor.

My wife, she was so nice and calm,
Just smiled, cleaned up the mess.
What I do tomorrow,
She said to me, is anybody's guess.

But I will keep you posted,
On things old people do.
Remember, when you get my age,
You'll do the same thing, too!

A Winner

I was at my finest,
Jabbing and dancing around.
That boy didn't have a chance.
Yessir, he was going down.

Had 'im backed up in the corner,
Had 'im against the wall.
I was sweating, my heart pounding,
I was having a ball.

I was bruised and battered,
Not recognizable one bit.
I was in a frenzy,
One more punch, one more hit.

"What in the world are you doing?!"
You said, "This was my boxing day."
"Oh, Dear Lord, won't you help me?"
I said, "PUT THE BOX AWAY."

Now I know the answer,
That's been gnawing at my gut.
What could I have been doing,
When I got that paper cut.

...It's just what old people do!

My daughter didn't quite understand this poem either. I have to admit, I had to remember exactly what happened that day. It seems there was a shadow of a stack of my wife's boxes and, thinking someone was in the house, haha, *I went after them!*

Strangers In My House

Who are these strangers in my house,
That have taken over my domain.
They never cease their endless chatter,
That drives me half insane.

They talk and chatter of endless things,
A lot of that I do not approve.
It is my habitat, my dwelling place,
I don't think I should be the one to move.

I really shouldn't let them offend me,
Irritate me and finally get my goat.
When I am the one who is sitting here,
Holding the dumb remote.

Love Getting Old

I just love getting old,
I'm not responsible for what I say or do.
It is amazing what I get by with,
Don't you wish that it were you?

I can say the dumbest things,
Make crazy gestures all I want.
I'll give you any answer,
Sometimes be pretty blunt.

I can scratch myself in public,
In places you wouldn't dare.
Don't have to fuss with how I look,
Care less about my hair.

All the while, I'm doggone happy,
Just watching folks and time go by.
That's just what us old folks do,
Before we up and die.

-Eat your heart out, you young people.
And have a great day! -Keith

A Little Fly

Did you ever stop to wonder,
What went on in the brains of a fly?
Does he wonder how long he might live,
Or when he might just up and die?

Does he actually possess,
Any brains at all?
Is there really anything,
In that tiny little skull?

Does he laugh when he annoys you?
Does he even really care?
Does it bother him one bit,
When he buzzed you in your hair?

I doubt it! He's just a little fly,
He is doing what little flies do.
He couldn't care less about me,
And cares even less about you.

So there is your lesson for today,
About the annoying little fly.
You ask me why I wrote this,
- I don't even know why!

Today I Wonder...

Did I tell my good wife I love her? Did I kiss her on the nose?
Did I help her count her fingers, after counting all her toes?

Did I brush my teeth today? Did I wash my face?
Do my shirt and blue jeans match? Did I dress in such a haste?

Did I let the old cat out? Did I empty out her box?
I couldn't let her come back in, I think I changed the locks.

Did I put the car in park? Will it roll back down the hill?
Did I take a double dose, of those doggone sleeping pills?

There are many things I wonder,
If I didn't do them or if I did.
Like, when I left the bathroom,
Did I put down the lid?

I guess I could keep going,
It will not change things one bit.
My kids are gonna look at me,
And say, *Dad is finally losing it.*

But that's okay, I love them,
They needn't be concerned at all.
I am out spending their inheritance...

And I am having myself a ball!

The End

Well, there you have my story,
Some things were added just for fun.
I hope it made your day complete,
After all your chores were done.

Perhaps some things made you feel real good,
And some things have made you grin.
Some may have made you shed a tear,
Or just gave you some peace within.

But they were written for a reason,
And I did have you in mind.
And now that it's all said and done,
It really was well worth my time.

Thank you,
Keith